Is That
The Library
Speaking?

Is That The Library Speaking?

by

KEN HORNSBY

ST. MARTIN'S PRESS
NEW YORK

ROBERT HALE LIMITED
LONDON

© *Ken Hornsby 1978*
First published in Great Britain 1978

ISBN 0 7091 6941 8

Robert Hale Limited
Clerkenwell House
Clerkenwell Green
London EC1

St. Martin's Press, Inc.,
175 Fifth Avenue
New York, N.Y. 10010

*First published in the United
States of America 1979*

Library of Congress Catalog
Card Number 78-604 65

ISBN 0-312-43728-5

Printed and bound in Great Britain
by Weatherby Woolnough, Wellingborough, Northants

Contents

Preface

After three weeks of tap-tap-tap-whirr-thump, tap-tap-tap-whirr-thump, it struck me that I was in the wrong job. The tap-tap-tap-whirr-thump was me on an ancient adding machine. I was working in the registration department of a large building firm in the City, at the start of a two-year course preparing me for a career as a company secretary. "A few months in every department to gain all-round working knowledge" was how the letter of appointment apologized for tucking me up in a dingy office, surrounded by six men, all aged upwards of fifty-five. (There's nothing wrong with being upwards of fifty-five; it's just that when you're only twenty-two yourself, you do feel a certain lack of oneness with your colleagues. Also I felt an even more certain lack of one-ness with the man who kept inviting me to "go driving" with him.)

I spent the days entering numbers in ledgers, tapping on the adding machine, and waiting for one o'clock, five-thirty, and the tea girl. It didn't seem much of a recipe for a challenging and fulfilling life. It took me three weeks to realize I couldn't stand it, and another four to work out my notice. The moment I decided to leave, I sat down to plan the future. I interviewed myself.

"Now you're a man of at least average intelligence," I began, flatteringly, "it shouldn't be above your powers of reasoning to work out for yourself exactly what you'd like to do. As a start, what *do* you like to do?" Rejecting answers like "Nothing", and "Watching the girl across the road getting dressed" and "Eating chocolate cake", I finally settled for "I like to read".

"Well then," continued the interviewer, "have you considered working with books?"

"At the library, you mean?" responded the interviewee, catching on quickly.

"Exactly so," said the interviewer, knowing instinctively his work was done.

It seemed a marvellous idea, I was bound to agree. It was near home, for one thing. No travelling, no fares, no dirty city. Also, so my memory told me, the atmosphere was peaceful and relaxed. It had an air of intellectuality about it. I could see myself there immediately: moving quietly about the bookshelves, placing the odd tome neatly in its place, looking things up, browsing, advising people on good reading.

Clearly, it was precisely what I was after. . . .

1

Resolution and Independence

It so happened I knew someone who had once worked in the library nearest to my home. I went to see him. "You realize," he said, "that the pay isn't very good?" Compared with the dust and the must of the city office, pay didn't seem particularly important, ". . . and that you'd be a junior – *my* junior?" he went on.

I hadn't realized that although Hugh had left that particular library, he was still working in the same borough; as a senior assistant at one of the branch libraries. Technically, I realized, I *would* be his junior. Despite the fact he was four days younger than me. Even that didn't seem to matter too much. There would be, after all, the browsing and the reading and the relaxed atmosphere.

"What do I do?"

"Just write to the chief librarian. You shouldn't have any trouble getting in. There aren't many young men going into the service these days. Specially with some sort of university education." (I had started a degree course at Oxford; unfortunately Latin and I hadn't hit it off too well and, not wishing to stay where I wasn't wanted, I had allowed myself to be sent down. Hugh was saying, in the sort of condescending way you can when you are four days younger, and two years senior, it might help a little.)

So I wrote to the chief librarian the kind of pompous letter you tend to write when you are twenty-two and looking for a job. Things like ". . . the sort of life and career opportunities it offers . . .", and ". . . would, of course, wish to follow the various courses open. . . ." I quickly received the offer of an interview.

I decided it would give an impression of worldliness and determination to Get On if I drove up for the interview in my old car (I knew enough about the geography of the library to know that the chief's office looked down on the road opposite). I therefore lurched up the road, parked rather publicly in a slightly dangerous place in order to be seen, got in and out several times, and walked over to the library, narrowly missing being run over by a bus.

As I entered, it seemed reassuringly familiar. As quiet and friendly as I had always known it when I had popped in on the way home from school. But when I asked the girl assistant to see the Chief Librarian, the atmosphere changed abruptly. I sensed a feeling of hostility positively radiate from her. (I discovered why, later. The only people who ask to see the chief are there to complain. I quickly learned to react the same way.) However, once I explained I actually had an appointment, and dispelled the conviction that I was about to slander each assistant in turn, she went to the switchboard, pressed a few knobs, and said, "Mr Hornsby is here to see you." Then she nodded (which seemed a curious way to reply on the telephone), put the phone down, and said to me that it was the first door on the right at the top of the stairs, and please go up.

I went up, and knocked. Absolutely nothing happened. I knocked again. Absolutely nothing happened again. I knocked a third time, and went in uninvited. The chief, who turned out to be someone quite different from the person I had always thought he was, turned round from the window and said "Ah, Beaver isn't it? Have you got the County lists?" I wasn't, and I hadn't. It was thoroughly unnerving. Furthermore, if his sight was that bad, I had wasted my time with the car. To say nothing of the parking ticket I was risking.

"I'm sorry," I started mumblingly, "I'm Hornsby."

"Ah yes, you were coming at ten o'clock, weren't you?" It was getting worse by the minute. I *had* come at ten. It was still only a minute past. I speculated on the effect of putting him right, but decided that as it would only have the result of making me seem as unpleasantly self-righteous as I actually felt, I'd let it go.

It obviously didn't matter much – for, as Hugh had said, it was clearly not going to be very difficult. The chief asked me what I liked reading, why, and various other even less important things; told me I would never be rich working in a library; and asked when I wanted to start.

I explained that I had three weeks' notice still to work out, and that I could begin on 5th November. I felt there was a joke lurking there somewhere, but it hardly seemed the right moment to pursue it.

He rang a bell and his secretary came in.

"Ah," he said, "you did say you wanted to go to night school, didn't you?" She didn't reply. While she wasn't replying, I wondered to myself whether the interview had been concluded, and whether I should quietly steal away. I also wondered idly why a middle-aged lady would be wanting to go to night school. Perhaps she was doing something really unexpected, like carpentry, or car maintenance. I began to warm to the sort of people who worked in libraries. Keen, enterprising people, who had wide-ranging interests, and were wide-awake to possibilities.

"Mr Hornsby – I'm sorry if I have caught you napping, but you did say you wanted to go to night school, didn't you?" I nodded, speechlessly.

"Miss Pirie, take Mr Hornsby into cataloguing and sort him out some staff library books. I hope you'll be very happy here. Come and see me if anything worries you. Good day."

Miss Pirie took me into the cataloguing department – a room I had never seen before, containing people I had never seen before. There were stacks of very old books about, and even larger stacks of very new ones. I was behind the scenes. I was given some books on librarianship, and walked out a budding librarian. The car wouldn't start, and I was grateful the chief was shortsighted.

2

The Joys of Shelving

At eight-forty-five on the 5th November I walked into the library in my business suit.

"I'm sorry Sir, we're not open to the public until half past nine" said the janitor. "Unless you want the reference library, and even that's not open until nine."

"No, actually I start work here today."

He looked surprised. (I realized why later; only fully-fledged librarians wore suits. Assistants didn't.) He showed me where to sign in.

"You sign here when you arrive, when you go off to lunch, when you return after lunch, and when you go home at night." The vision of the peaceful, enlightened atmosphere receded a little.

At this moment a very small thin man appeared.

"My name's Beaver," he squeaked, in an extraordinarily high-pitched voice.

I thought, "Good gracious, if the chief mistook me for him he must be amazingly short-sighted." Then a further thought struck me. Could he see to read?

"Signed in, have you?" Beaver squeaked again. "Come along, I'll show you the staff room where you can put your coat, then we'll start."

After I had put my coat away, he led me downstairs again. He took me towards the counter which separated the assistants from the public.

"The counter," he explained, pointing at it. It was easy to believe. It did, after all, look exactly like a counter. I nodded, waiting for the next vital piece of information. As none was forthcoming, I looked at Beaver to see what was to happen next.

He however was looking at me, clearly waiting for a reaction. I looked more closely at it. It was made of a dirty sort of pine, much like thousands of other counters up and down the country. I couldn't for the life of me think of anything to say about it. It looked like a counter; Beaver had said it was a counter; and I could do nothing but agree. I nodded. "Right," I said, just to make it perfectly clear I had understood.

Beaver looked disappointed. He had apparently expected me to be overwhelmed with excitement.

"It's where we work," he said, giving the whole thing up, and speaking in as low-pitched a voice as he could muster, though still several notes above that of the girl in the amply-filled yellow blouse talking into the telephone. As that seemed even more obvious than the first fact he had imparted, I contented myself with a nod this time. Coming to the conclusion that this conversation was going nowhere, he changed the subject abruptly, and surprisingly.

"Let's start with some shelving," he said, turning away. I decided I would try to repair my bad impression by entering into the spirit of his joke with fervour.

"Fine," I said. "Absolutely. There's nothing like postponing things for making a good start on a Monday morning." Beaver looked so blank at this he looked really stupid (which didn't require a great effort on his part.)

"Shelving is putting books on shelves," he said, in an effort to recover the situation and put some apparently much-needed sense into the conversation. "Come along."

I followed him out of the counter area towards the fiction department, and where I knew lived the shelves on which the books which had just been returned were placed.

There were several youngish people there, all feverishly pulling books from these 'returned' shelves. Two of them were girls, and judging by the barely concealed giggles, they had heard the entire dialogue between

14

Beaver and me. Beaver continued with the lesson.

"These are the books which came back on Saturday. We're now putting them in their right places on the right shelves, in alphabetical order. A-B-C . . ." he added finally, to dispel any further confusion I might be experiencing. "If you'd like to take the R–Zs, you can start shelving them."

It sounds childishly easy. You simply extract from the returned shelves all the books with authors whose names began with anything from R to Z. I took a quick look at the others. Their arms were going in and out like an octopus in a fight. Each time they grabbed a book and deposited it in their free arm. "Right," I thought to myself. "Go." The very first book my eyes lighted on was by Simenon. The second by Thomas. The third by Waugh. The fourth by Trafford. All the books seemed to be mine. In fact just about all the books *were* mine – for the simple reason that by now all the rest had been extracted.

I took an armful and walked over to my shelves. I took hold of the Simenon, found the Ss, and stuck it between two other Simenons. I took the book by Thomas and found that just where it ought to go there was a large book by someone called Tuffness named *The Pursuit and Capture of Rhinoceros*. It didn't sound like fiction, and I knew enough to tell that as it had a number on the spine, it was definitely non-fiction.

Feeling a little smug, I decided to put right the error of an inefficient library assistant. I put my armful of fiction down on the floor and set off with the errant book to find its correct place.

Unfortunately I rapidly found that I was not as knowledgeable about the numbering system as I had thought, and I soon got lost behind some distant shelves, looking rather hopelessly for a series of books with a seven-figure number. While I was searching I heard a door open and a voice I had heard before say "Good morning". The other assistants all said "Good morning" back, and then there was a crash, a "Damn," and the sound of a body landing on the floor. It was the chief, and he had fallen over my pile of books.

"Beaver," shouted the cross voice, "what's going on? Why are these books shelved on the floor?" I was in a dilemma. Should I stay hidden and hope it would all pass, or come out and try to explain? A high-pitched whine told me that Beaver was winding himself up to say something, but judging by the uncertainty of the sound, actual words still seemed some way off. There was only one thing to do under the circumstances, and I did it. I stayed where I was.

"It's not good enough. Books live on shelves, not floors," said the chief, and he stumped off.

I still hadn't found my number, and a quick look round the shelves confirmed the fact that I wasn't going to find it. I didn't feel like asking anyone, particularly Beaver himself, who by now must be hot on my trail anyway. I quickly formed a plan which, though not tinged with the highest motives, certainly offered itself as an easy escape. Why not just put the book anywhere in the non-fiction shelves? It would be out of my way in the R–Zs, and if not in the right place, it would at least be in the non-fiction where it belonged. Accordingly I rather shamefacedly pushed it in among some books on cats. They *were* animals, at least.

I went back to my fiction, now lying on a windowsill being looked over by an irritated Beaver. I walked up quietly; too quietly, because when I arrived he jumped and squawked like a castrated hyena. (I hadn't actually heard a castrated hyena squawk, but surrounded by the millions of words in a public library I found my metaphors running away with me. I was pretty sure that was what a castrated hyena would sound like.)

After the squawk he enquired where I had been. I explained about the rhinoceros book.

"I expect one of the other assistants put it there by mistake," I ended, not without pride at having discovered the error.

"Why?" asked Beaver sharply.

"I can't imagine – I don't expect it was done on purpose," I said magnanimously.

"I mean, why do you think one of the assistants did it?"

"Well . . . who else?" I asked lamely.

"The public," said Beaver triumphantly.

I was not yet used to the idea that the public were a different race; strictly over-the-counter people who did odd things and asked odd questions.

"But why?" I asked.

"Because that's where they were standing. Unless it was a juvenile."

I was beginning to find this terminology a bit of a strain. First when Beaver said Public I had thought he was referring to the 'Spotted Dog' nearby, and now I presumed that juvenile was short for juvenile delinquent (I wasn't so far wrong, I was soon to discover, in that respect). In fact I learned it was just the official term for children.

"Honestly," said Beaver, "you can't imagine some of the things they get up to. Rearranging books, leaving them on windowsills, taking them out without tickets." While Beaver was going on about the iniquities of the reading public I was remembering something I had done as a child in that very room.

In this library, as in all others, the books were lined up with the front of the shelves. When smaller, I had thought, with rare consideration for others, what a tremendous job this must be for the assistants. Why not, I had wondered to myself, align the books with the *back* of the shelves? It would still look tolerably neat, and would save a great deal of tidying. It had then occurred to me with typical schoolboy humility that probably the assistants hadn't thought of it, and that it would be rather nice of me to drop a gentle hint. Accordingly I methodically went along a complete row of shelves, pushing in all the books to align with the back of the shelves. But next time I came back to the library I saw that they were level with the front again. "If at first . . ."

I had thought, and for about three months I had waged this war of nerves with the authorities. In the end I had to admit that I had lost.

"Why, I remember about six years ago we had a particular spate of books being pushed to the backs of the shelves. We're always getting the odd shelf done – but this went on for about three months. It used to drive Shirley mad. It was always *her* books," Beaver went on inexorably. "She thought it was something personal in the end."

"Oh no," I exclaimed, "I'm sure it wasn't."

"Are you?" said Beaver, looking a trifle bewildered.

"It seems incredible," I said, wondering how to get out of the particular knot I had got myself into. "The things people do. . . ."

"Anyway," said Beaver, "you'd better be getting on with this fiction."

Putting about 150 books in their right alphabetical places doesn't sound too difficult. But there were, I quickly discovered, complications. First there was, on just about every shelf, a book that didn't belong there. My book on rhinoceros was typical. Then quite often a complete shelf-full was so disarranged that I had to take them all off and start from scratch. Sometimes I would end up with two sequences. This happened easily. You only had to put a 'Thomas' next to another 'Thomas', and a 'Thomerton' next to that, and then to find that the original 'Thomas' was in the wrong place, to get yourself in a total state of disarray. It happened all the time.

When I had eventually put all my fiction books away, the state of my shelves was unbelievable. Several of them had books for about only half their length. Others were so tightly jammed that not a single leaf extra could have been got in. In fact, it would have been hard to get a leaf out. I looked at the shelves that already had been done by my new colleagues. They looked perfect. Every book tidy. Every shelf full – but not too full. Everything in order. I looked at mine. They looked as though they

The Joys of Shelving

had been done over by a poltergeist. Clearly, I hadn't finished with shelving. Even though we had started with it.

I realized that a figure of doom was behind me. It was Beaver, breathing hard. He had presumably not yet got over the chief's collapse on the floor, but I felt he needn't have looked quite so disagreeable.

"Bit untidy, aren't they?" he observed.

"Bit," I said guardedly, waiting for his next move. Beaver became businesslike.

"You'll have to spread the load somewhat. Ease out the full shelves, and you'll find the empty ones will fill up." It hadn't taken me thirteen years of education, during at least ten of which I had studied mathematics, not to realize that without being told.

"You'll find that there is nearly always the right *total* amount; it's just that they need spreading." Beaver went away, with small strides and big trousers aflap.

I noticed by now that the Public were in. That is to say, there were two elderly women sitting on the window-sill talking about their rates of pay. They were both wearing scarves around their heads, like turbans, and both looked tired. One had a book in her hands, closed. The other wasn't even making that much of a gesture; she was quite unashamedly resting. The fact that it was a public library she was in was quite irrelevant as far as she was concerned. She was tired, and she was resting. There was by now no sign of the other assistants. Beaver had consigned himself to the counter – which meant he was attending to the public. Taking in their books and stamping the new ones with the date when they were due back. In fact at the moment no-one was either coming or going, and Beaver was reading an old copy of the *Children's Newspaper*. A fact I found psychologically interesting.

I looked again at my shelves. I noticed a curious fact. There was never an empty shelf next to a full one. This appeared to be an invariable rule. In order to ease one shelf, one had to re-arrange at least two, and usually three, other shelves to reach a slack one.

I started on the onslaught. I found out another thing about books. They were exceedingly dirty. After about five minutes of this, when I had succeeded in sorting out one crush, my hands were distinctly grubby and had a nasty feel about them – as though I had been gardening – which I hate. I pressed on, re-arranging for all I was worth. After about a lifetime and a half, I had all my books tidy. I went up to Beaver.

"I've finished that lot," I said, not without pride.

"Ah, splendid," said Beaver, "let's start on the non-fiction, shall we? You can have the seven hundreds."

I don't think Beaver could ever have imagined what that brief sentence meant to me. I had been thinking, as I finished the fiction, that the arranging and tidying of books was presumably the job that everyone hated and had to be got out of the way as quickly as possible. And then one started being a librarian, at approximately ten o'clock each day. So when I had walked up to Beaver, light was my tread and hopeful my heart. And then, with one easy remark, I was back tidying again.

I realized that Beaver had meant all the non-fiction that came into the sphere of books with 7 . . . on their spines. I walked over to the non-fiction shelves – the returned books section again. At this moment I caught sight of my colleagues again. They were all busily putting the last tidying touches to their respective non-fiction shelves. And all very neat they looked too – with the notable exception of the seven hundreds, which seemed also to have had a visit from that poltergeist.

Despite the fact that the other assistants had presumably taken their books away from the returned shelves, there were an enormous number of books still there. In my rapidly developing pessimistic outlook, I presumed every one must be mine. In fact, I received the first nice shock since I had been in the place. They *weren't* all mine. There were a lot of one hundreds, and a lot of nine hundreds – and a lot more of seven hundreds.

I took up an armful and set off to my shelves. I found
that the non-fiction could be both better and worse
than the fiction. Some sections seemed hardly to have
been touched at all. And others got a tremendous going-
over. It was inevitable, of course, that the seven
hundreds were among those which had been most
stampeded. I found too that they were even more complicated to sort out than the fiction. Some of the
numbers became so involved it was almost impossible to
be sure that they were going back into the right places
even when you were concentrating. And by now I was
so punch-drunk, I wasn't. I found several books in the
wrong place completely – among them, of course, my
book on rhinoceros. I was utterly stymied with this one.
I could either leave it, which seemed rather feeble, or
else – inspired thought – put it back on the returned
shelves for the 500-er to put away next morning. This
was brilliant. Already I had discovered a way to get out
of trouble when I was nonplussed. Not that I was a
habitual putter-off, but it was always useful to know a
way. I put the wretched book back on the returned
shelves and turned away. Behind me was Beaver. I had
no idea beavers were so friendly. Beaver was everywhere.

"Why," he asked, "are you putting a book *back*? Have
you finished reading it?" He was getting quite sarcastic.
It wasn't reasonable on the first day. He pontificated:
"When we find a book on our shelves that doesn't
belong to us, we put it in the right place. We don't just
get rid of it. It's got to go back sometime, hasn't it?"

I decided to be straight. "Yes, of course. The only
thing is – I seem to get a bit lost with some of these
numbers. Could you rescue me?" This, I discovered, was
a most advantageous move. Apparently Beaver had
been waiting all morning for me to ask for help. He
loved helping. He loved appearing efficient, useful, helpful, kind, encouraging. Anything, in fact, which boosted
his ego, he liked.

"Yes, of course, *Ken*," he said, smiling seraphically.

He really said "Ken" as though it were underlined. It was his 'be nice to the troops' act. He led me through the shelves to where the rhinoceros book belonged, and thrust it triumphantly home.

"Never be afraid to ask, Ken," he said, very loudly for the benefit of the two ladies on the windowsill. He walked off. Immediately, he walked back.

"Ken . . ." he began rather hesitantly, "Er, you did do the R–Zs, didn't you?"

I nodded, suspecting something nasty was coming.

"Oh, then would you like to come along with me, and I'll show you how to tidy them."

I was beginning to feel rather ill-disposed towards Beaver. I had found it interesting – indeed I had got a rather superior feeling of pleasure in finding out – that he wanted to be helpful. But to offer to show me how to tidy books was really rather unnecessary I felt. Particularly when I had already done it. But I had no option. He was already *en route* for the fiction department and I had to trail along behind him. As we walked I began to feel really resentful. I was the new boy; right. I had to be shown round; right again. But to be shown solemnly how to tidy up books was an uncalled-for piece of ostentatious superiority on his part. But at least I had the insight to keep quiet.

"This is what we do," started Beaver, pulling all the books from the shelf one inch out from the front of it. "Then we just run the back of the hand along them, and they flush themselves with the front of the shelf." I found Beaver's description amusing in a way he had never intended. I smiled. Beaver saw me.

"I know there doesn't appear to be anything to it, but before you get too carried away, just you try it. Then perhaps you won't think it so funny." In fact he didn't sound so schoolmasterish as the words imply. He wasn't even mildly reprimanding me for laughing. I looked at Beaver's shelf, then at my own. There really didn't seem to be much difference. I thought I would try a sly one.

"Well, thank you very much," I said, "I'll remember that for next time."

Beaver looked at me suspiciously, not sure whether I was trying to be clever or not.

"Yes, O.K. – don't bother to go over them all again now; they don't look too bad," he said, still looking puzzled. "If you like to finish the non-fiction," he went on, "we can then go up to tea."

I am not particularly fond of tea. But when we finally reached the tea-room it tasted as good as whisky.

3

The Lady with a Lapdog

After tea, Beaver led me downstairs and, ceremoniously, into the 'counter'; an area about twelve feet square, almost totally surrounded by the dirty pine counter that had failed to excite me the last time Beaver had pointed it out. We worked in the centre, and the readers milled around outside. It felt very public, to be in that private area. For years I had visited that library as a member of the public. Now I was in the goldfish bowl, instead of feeding it.

"This is Jim Chiltern," said Beaver, introducing me to a large pimply youth of about eighteen, "and this is Jill Shaw." Jill was about the same age, but a lot smaller, with red hair and, as far as I could see, no pimples. Beaver explained how the tickets were filed, and left me to it, with Chiltern vaguely watching over me.

I waited in trepidation for the first customer to come in. I didn't have to stand around long, for within seconds in walked a fierce-looking woman with a dachshund in her arms, and about eight books in a bag. My heart already somewhere in the region of my socks, I turned round for Chiltern.

He was walking away to find a book for a red-faced youth who looked as if he were perfectly able to find a book for himself. Jill Shaw was busy with a small queue of people waiting for her to stamp their books out. But she looked across and whispered frantically, "No dogs," and turned back to her customers.

I was beginning to feel hot under the collar. Where, for instance, was Beaver, who was supposed – surely – to be keeping an eye on me? A high-pitched cough from the stockroom gave me the answer to that.

"I'm sorry . . ." I began tentatively, "no dogs are allowed in."

"Nonsense," retorted the dowager, "I shall carry her." I hadn't the faintest idea whether that made it all right or not. I looked at Jill, but could only see a back. Chiltern had disappeared completely. The stockroom was still coughing.

"Come along, young man, come along. Here are my books. I shall carry Susan as I always do."

Here, at any rate, seemed to be an answer. The dog question was settled. That was assuming she always *did* carry the dog. There didn't appear much I could do about finding out, so I set my mind to the books. She hadn't been particularly helpful about them. She had, it is true, taken them out of her bag, but that was all. They faced all ways; they were shut; one had the cover flapping off.

I took the first one, and found that it was overdue; that was a complication for a start. Overdue tickets worked in a different way from the others. There were only a few, all filed in just three trays. I found the right place, but the ticket wasn't there. By now I was thoroughly bemused. Another client came, and queued behind the first. A sudden and prolonged buzzing proclaimed the fact that the phone was ringing. I was by now very unhappy indeed. I decided to ignore that first book for a moment, in the hope that Chiltern would be back to help, and press on with the second. That was also overdue; also not in its tray. Similarly with the third. I simply couldn't understand it. A third client came in; I had quite a queue. The fourth book was due back on a different day – not overdue – and, joy of joys, the ticket was in the right place. The fifth book was exactly the same. The sixth was overdue – but a different date again. And it was there in the right place. The last two had only gone out three days previously, but they too were in their rightful places.

The phone seemed to have been buzzing for ever. Jill

was making no attempt to answer it (I later discovered she never did), and Chiltern hadn't come back. I looked at the switchboard, which was also located within the counter, and I saw a ridiculous little white eye winking at me, and two little prongs moving up and down in time with the ringing tone. I hadn't the faintest idea how to answer it, and anyway the lady with the dachshund was looking very impatient.

Things were looking really desperate when Beaver came in. He marched up to the telephone switchboard, flipped one lever, and the buzzing miraculously stopped.

"All right?" he said to me.

"Can't find these," I muttered, pointing to the delinquent books.

"Overdue juveniles," he prompted, going over to the second in my queue.

Of course I should have realized that the J before the number of the books meant juvenile, and that they were filed separately. Sure enough, they were in the right place. I next had to calculate the fines due. I made it four books overdue – two by one week, and two by two. That came to eighteen pence.

"Eighteen pence, please," I said in as businesslike fashion as possible.

"Eighteen pence? Whatever for?"

"These four books overdue."

"Overdue – let me see."

"Look – two for the tenth, and two for the eighteenth."

With rather ill-grace, she gave me a fifty pence piece. I found the change, gave her her receipt tickets (which she ignored), and took her books.

Beaver had by now disposed of the other two waiting clients, and was on the phone. Chiltern had come back, and Jill was doing nothing.

"Been busy?" enquired Chiltern hopefully.

Jill shook her head. I didn't know whether I had been busy or just inefficient. I suspected just inefficient. I speculated as to how long it would take me to get used to the counter.

Suddenly I saw the lady with the dachshund. She was in the children's library, and the dog was rolling on the floor on its back.

"I told you no dogs," said Jill, grinning maliciously.

"Who let that dog in?" asked Beaver, now off the phone.

"I did – she said she always carried it," I answered, feeling rather feeble. Beaver was unexpectedly nice about it.

"I know, it is rather difficult with her – she's a member of the Library Committee anyway," he said. "Still, you'd better go and tell her she's either got to pick it up or pitch it out." This little piece of rhetoric had clearly pleased Beaver, for he smiled as he ended. I walked over to her.

"Er, you did say you were going to carry it . . ." I started.

"*It?*" she boomed. "She's a bitch. A pedigree bitch. She's got breeding."

Which seemed to be more than one could claim for her owner, I thought.

"I'm very sorry," I said, realizing what a bad start I had made, "but even so, you did say you were going to carry her. Dogs aren't really allowed in the library."

"I hope you aren't going to try to tell me the rules of this library, young man. I am on the Library Committee and I help to make them."

It was on the tip of my tongue to ask, "Why don't you keep them then?" In fact it was so much on the tip of my tongue that I did say, "Well, I think you really ought to keep to them particularly in that case."

She took one look at me and said loudly, "I wish to see Mr Mortimore."

Things were getting right out of hand. This morning was little short of disastrous, it seemed to me. We walked up to the counter. I told Beaver that she wanted to see the chief.

"I'm afraid Mr Mortimore isn't available this morning, Mrs Bell," said Beaver.

"He must be available. He's a public servant, isn't he?"

"Yes madam, but his job is running the library service in this borough, and at this moment he is in conference with the branch librarians discussing next week's book purchases. Can I help you?"

Mrs Bell obviously realized there was nothing satisfactory to be gained by pursuing that line any more, so she turned to me.

"This young man has been extremely rude to me; I would be glad if you would reprimand him, and get him to apologize to me."

"What happened, Mrs Bell?" asked Beaver more wearily than I would have expected.

"Well, first of all he called Susan *it*, and then he said that if I help to make the rules here, I should be ready to keep them." Mrs Bell clearly realized as she spoke that this was in fact doing her no good at all. I shouldn't have put it quite like that, obviously – but obviously too there was much in my argument.

"What was my colleague referring to?" asked Beaver. My respect for him had already gone up; to be referred to as his colleague was really rather nice of him.

"It was Susan; she was rolling on the floor." This didn't sound too good for Mrs Bell, either. She began to look rather embarrassed.

"Look," she went on, "I'm prepared to forget the whole thing. . . ."

Beaver, however, wasn't. On his home ground, Beaver was king. And the fact that Mrs Bell was on the Library Committee didn't daunt him at all.

"We've had this before, haven't we, Mrs Bell? You know dogs aren't allowed in. Now, you will either have to take her out, or hold her."

"Just supposing I do take her out, where can I leave her? Is there an assistant available to mind her?"

"No, Mrs Bell, you can tie her up to the banisters if you like, providing she doesn't whine too loudly."

"Susan does *not* whine," retorted Mrs Bell angrily,

"and I will not tie her to the banisters. I shall leave." And without another word, she swept out, carrying a book in her hand. Beaver heaved a sigh, said something decidedly blasphemous, and shot after her. There was a long silence, and a long absence of Beaver. Other people came in; other people went out. I found most tickets; Chiltern had to help with a few. Then Beaver came back. He looked tired, cross, and triumphant. In his hand he held the book.

"I know her," he said. "If I hadn't got that book, we'd never have seen it again."

"D'you mean she'd have stolen it?" I asked incredulously.

"Not stolen exactly; she would just have said, if she had been found out, that we never reminded her when it was due back. And as she shot off without booking it out, *we'd* never have known she had it anyway. And if she ever admitted to it, she would have said how lax we were letting people get through without booking them out properly. She's a real so-and-so. No principles at all, but never stops talking about them. She's only on the Library Committee because she's not qualified to do anything else."

I wondered how typical Mrs Bell was of the people we had to deal with. Surely most people weren't as awkward.

"Good morning," I heard a gruff, foreign voice behind me say. "I vish to renew my pooks."

"Have you them here?" asked Chiltern.

"No."

"Have you the numbers, then?"

"No. But vun vos green, and vun is by Hellenski."

"We must have the numbers."

"Well – they were due pack today." The old man sounded rather desperate. "I can't come all this way again."

Chiltern answered: "Well, that's all right. Just ring up and tell us the numbers. That'll do."

"So very kind," said the old man, shuffling out. A

minute later he shuffled back.

"Vot is your telephone number?" he asked.

"It's inside the books," said Chiltern.

"Oh – but I haven't got the pooks. My vife has them in Germany. That's why I vant to renew them." I wondered how he was going to give us the numbers by phone when the books were in Germany. Chiltern had obviously realized that too, but had a masterful trick up his sleeve. He handed the man a piece of paper.

"Here's the phone number." And that was all he said.

I thought it was just as well I couldn't answer the phone, because whoever did was going to have a rather difficult ten minutes.

That was the last notable thing that happened before lunch, which was just as well, for I was dropping. One of the things I hadn't taken into consideration when I had my vision of the dreamy, intellectual atmosphere of the library was the fact that assistants spend practically the whole of their working hours on their feet. And I was nearly out on mine!

4

The Tramp and Tovey

After I had been home for lunch, at precisely two o'clock I entered the arena again, feeling a little more confident than I had in the morning. None of the people inside the counter were among those I had met in the morning, but before any introductions could be made, in wandered a tramp and leaned across the counter confidentially towards me.

"*Children's Newspaper?*" he enquired.

I was immediately thrown off balance. I remembered seeing Beaver reading it earlier, but I had no idea where it lived. I looked round for help. A girl I hadn't yet met was turning the handle of the switchboard, and the other two – both men – were dealing with other ustomers. I cast my eyes rather hopelessly about, until I ad a sudden inspiration. The reading room. There were zens of papers there, many clipped to reading boards, many others lying around in hard covers. It was the obvious place.

"In the reading room," I said happily, pleased with my deduction. The tramp shook his head. I thought he must be deaf.

"IN THE READING ROOM," I said, more firmly.

"No," said the tramp.

Not to be outdone, "Yes," I said. I detected the first signs of weakening.

"You sure?" he asked.

"Yes," I said, beginning to feel less sure.

"Hrreuch," said the tramp, and drooped off towards the reading room.

A few other people came in, and I had a fairly successful time finding their tickets.

"You must be Ken," said a voice suddenly.

"Yes," I replied, truthfully.

"I'm Tovey – the Lending Librarian. You met my deputy, Beaver, this morning. And this is Bill Davies."

Tovey I had never seen before. I interpreted his curious title as meaning he was in charge of the lending library. Bill Davies I had seen many times. In fact, until I discovered the chief was someone else, I had assumed Bill *was* the chief. (I found out, later, that half the borough was under that impression; something which Bill made no attempt to discourage.) He was tall, distinguished, and rather military in bearing. He also had a pungent smell of pipe tobacco about him, and (again as I discovered later) an urgent desire to do no work at all. Tovey was also tall; considerably less distinguished; looked, and was, easy-going.

"And this here," added Tovey in an avuncular way, "is young Janet."

Young Janet, while by no means a beauty, was definitely one of the better things I had seen that day. Not much more than a schoolgirl, she had a most engaging grin. While I was being engaged by it, I suddenly found myself also looking at the tramp.

"Children's Newspaper?" he asked, tonelessly. I was beginning to get irritated.

"Yes?"

"Can I have it?"

"In the reading room – I told you."

"No."

"Yes."

"No."

"Wait," I said. He obviously couldn't see too well. Tovey was on the phone. Janet busy. No-one else coming in on my side.

"I'm just going into the reading room to find a paper for this gentleman," I mouthed at Mr Tovey. He nodded, absently.

"Come on," I said to the tramp, and marched into the reading room to end the problem. As I had never been in there before, I didn't really know where to start. All I could actually do was turn over every paper until I found it. This didn't go down too well with those people who were reading them, but on the whole they accepted me as a member of the staff doing something tiresome but necessary. I went around fifty-three papers. No *Children's Newspaper*. What now? I asked myself.

"It's kept under the counter, so that the children don't steal it," said the tramp, irritatingly.

This was a nasty one. I decided to come clean. I put on an air of honest frankness, mixed with easy charm.

"Well, that settles that," I simpered. "Do you know, this is my very first afternoon here. I've obviously still got a lot to learn." The tramp looked solemnly at me and, after a certain amount of cogitation, said "Hrreuch" again and vanished.

"I see you've been making friends," said Tovey, materializing at my elbow. "Now – would you like to go upstairs and have a cup of tea?"

I saw Janet ahead of me on the stairs, and I followed her into the staff room, in which I found Jill already seated, reading.

Janet poured two teas, took one, and settled herself down. She got out a book and started to read. A dead silence occupied the room.

I didn't like this very much. Here was I, and here were two girls, and a total silence. It didn't seem right. I cast about in my mind for some conversation. Hadn't I read somewhere that a librarian had to have very wide tastes, and no particular interests? In fact, take it to its logical conclusion, and one could say it was better if he didn't read at all.

"I have heard," I ventured, "that librarians shouldn't read themselves."

"What should they read then?" asked Jill, cattily. Janet lifted her head, smiled faintly, and returned to her book.

"Ah," I said, wisely.

There didn't, after all, seem very much else to say.

5

Problem Puddles

At the end of ten minutes, I looked at my watch, looked at the two girls, looked at my watch again, and sighed heavily. There was no response.

Cornily, I said, "Well. . . ." Still no response. Not even a sigh or another "Well". I didn't feel I should overrun my time on my first day, no matter what the 'professionals' were doing. I put my cup down, got myself up, and started for the door. At this, Jill started to speak. Aha, I thought; conscience – aided by my getting up – had pricked her into action.

"We wash our own cups up," she said.

I washed, dried, departed crestfallen – and a trifle bewildered. They were taking an unfairly long tea-break, and it didn't seem right. (They weren't, in fact, I realized later. They were both working until eight-fifteen, while I was finishing at five. This meant they had half-an-hour, instead of ten minutes, for tea.)

But as I walked down the stairs, events were in progress which quickly drove the iniquities of the girls from my mind. There had clearly been a happening. In place of the relatively quiet library I had left ten minutes before, there was now a remarkable and uncharacteristic din going on. There was a lot of shouting, a lot of feet running about, a lot of people at the counter. I pushed past a crowd of children, and forced my way into the counter area.

"Whatever's happened?" I asked Mr Tovey.

"I don't know, what *has* happened?" he replied in a rather surprised voice.

"All the commotion – it sounds like we've been invaded."

"Oh, you mean the children? It's a quarter past four. They're on their way home from school."

I hadn't realized until that moment that they were all children. And indeed, Mr Tovey spoke the truth. I myself used regularly to come into that very library on my way home from school. Presumably the same school, although I couldn't believe we had behaved like that.

I took a look into the children's room. It was total pandemonium. There must have been about fifty of them, in a room only about five yards by ten – and open at the top of each wall so that the noise carried uninterrupted all over the adult library sections. How did children, I wondered, presumably tired after a hard day ruining several teachers' lives, turn into such a marauding band? The sight of this seething wriggling mass was terrifying. Thank goodness I was no longer a child having to fight my way through it all. No power on earth would get me in that room.

"Go and see if you can quieten them down a bit, will you?"

That was Tovey, employing unknown techniques of treachery in reading my thoughts. I stepped tentatively towards the children's library, and looked round for moral support. Inexplicably, neither Jill nor Janet had reappeared. There was nothing for it.

I walked in, hoping the mere presence of a member of the staff might have a suitable quelling effect. In fact I might equally well have been invisible. No-one took the remotest notice, with the notable exception of one six-year-old who asked me if I had seen her sister. I hadn't. At least I didn't think I had. What did she look like? But by the time I had organized my thoughts in this direction, the child had rushed off unheeding. So what was I to do?

The natural temptation was to shout out "Shut up the lot of you!" However, this didn't seem to me to be quite sophisticated enough for a library. Anyway, even though the children were making no attempt to observe the 'Silence' sign, I felt that *I* shouldn't disregard it too blatantly.

"Could you be a little quieter?" I ventured, in what I considered a fairly good imitation of measured school-masterly tones. This was totally ineffectual.

"A bit less noise please," I tried again. Still no effect. I decided to ask for help.

"What do you do with them?" I asked Tovey, baffled.

"Ah, we'll soon sort them out," he said, grinning.

"SHUT UP THE LOT OF YOU!" he bellowed. This produced a fairly satisfactory silence.

"See if you can start tidying up a bit, will you, and generally keep an eye on them."

So far as I could see from a brief survey, both orders were totally impracticable. Compared with the state of the children's books, the seven hundreds had been as untouched by human hand. Also, many of the small children's books were very tall and very thin, with no name on the binding. So any question of easy restoration to order – alphabetical or otherwise – was largely out of the question. (I discovered in time that the other assistants never really bothered with these books; they just made them *look* tidy. After all, they reasoned, if the little children only take the books for the pictures, what is the sense of arranging the authors in alphabetical order? A good point, I decided, and adopted it the first day I heard of it.)

As for the children themselves, Mr Tovey's carefully chosen and profound words had not exactly left a lasting impression. Or to put it another way, Babel had re-turned. I thought I'd try it.

"SHUT UP THE LOT OF YOU!"

"Do you always copy him?" a small boy enquired conversationally.

I began to prowl around, pushing gently between pairs of children. Slowly my continued presence began to be felt. The noise subsided a little, the running slowed, fewer books flew across the room. I was feeling

37

quite cheered, when I came upon it.

It was a puddle. Just a small puddle, but unmistakably wet and childish. And in the corner, a small boy looking silent and guilty. He was only about six, and seemed as though he didn't know what to do next. I didn't quite know what to do next, either.

"Have you finished?" I asked thoughtfully. He nodded, eyes downcast.

"Are you with someone?" He nodded again.

"Who?"

But that was as far as I could get. Overwhelmed by the enormity of his achievement, he could provide no further information. Some of the other children were beginning to go by now, and none of those remaining seemed to be attached to him.

It then occurred to me that, small as he was, it was more than likely he had a parent with him in the adult library. All I had to do was find her. This was less easy than it sounds. By now most of the children had departed, and so had most of the noise. This meant that my question would be heard by all. Which made it rather difficult to go up to every likely looking adult and enquire clearly, "Have you got a child that might have caused a puddle?"

So I started my detective work by just looking at the women dotted around to see which looked parental. I selected the most likely one, and made a meaning face at her. It was, I thought, a fairly easy face to understand, which said clearly, "Have you a child in there? If so, could you accompany me into the children's library for a moment while I have a word with you both?" No reaction. I tried again, harder.

She looked back, and then walked away from the returned book shelves to an out-of-the-way section. I thought she must have got half the message, and I followed her.

"Excuse me," I began confidentially, "but I'm afraid there's a little trouble with your small boy . . ."

"Are you sure?" she asked.

"Afraid so; quite sure. The *evidence* is there."

"Only, you see, I haven't got a small boy." I retreated, confused. I decided that I needed help again, so I approached Mr Tovey.

"There's a puddle . . ." I began.

"Yes, I've seen it. See if you can find the mother, would you?"

"You haven't any idea who it is, have you?" I asked hopefully.

"I can't really recognize one puddle from the next," said Tovey, displaying his wit again. I thought I'd ignore that.

"That's the culprit, over there."

"Little so-and-so," said Tovey. "No, I've no idea." There was nothing for it but to try again. I walked back into the adult section and looked around. I selected another vaguely matriarchal-looking woman, and employed my 'face' again. She snorted.

"Excuse me," I mouthed, "could I have a word with you?"

"Certainly," she replied, in a surprisingly resonant voice, "What is it?"

"Could you come over here?"

"Why, whatever for?"

"Well, it's a little private."

She turned back to the shelves, grabbed about half a dozen books she had clearly had her eye on, and stepped back to talk to me.

"I'm sorry to bother you, but is that your small boy in there?"

"Which one?"

"About six, with a red jersey on."

"Show me."

I led her into the children's library. The child had vanished.

"That's odd. He seems to have vanished," I said, rather feebly. "Only he left a puddle, and I'm trying to find his mother."

"Well, he doesn't seem to be here now, does he? It

looks as if your problem has departed," she said. I could only agree. Except that part of the problem remained; namely the evidence itself.

"Sorry for bothering you," I said, and went over to Mr Tovey to see what to do next.

"Shall I tell the janitor?" I asked, thinking it was about time I took the initiative. "Presumably he's the one to mop it up."

"Yes, you try," said Tovey with a smile. "You'll find him down in the basement. Through that door, and then follow the pin-ups." That sounded like a part of the reference library I hadn't bargained for. I went through the door, and down the stairs – sure enough following the pin-ups. I wondered if Mr Mortimore ever went down there.

"Perhaps he goes quite often," I thought to myself, smiling. I found Mr Stewart, the janitor, reading the *Daily Mirror*. I explained about the puddle, and asked if he would mop it up.

"Oh. Ah. Well. Is it in the library?" It seemed a slightly absurd question. Yes, it was in the library.

"Only I'm not supposed to walk around there while we're open. The boss doesn't like overalls."

"Oh, it's all right," I hastened to explain. "Mr Tovey asked me to ask you."

"Oh. Ah. Well. It's my leg. War."

I was beginning to realize why Mr Tovey had smiled so knowingly. I also realized that if I didn't assert myself here and now, I'd never get him to do anything in the future.

"Look, Mr Stewart," I started determinedly, "there's a puddle and it needs wiping up and you're the janitor."

"You're new, aren't you?"

I didn't see what that had to do with it, but yes, I had to admit, I was new.

". . . only this is my rest time, you see."

"It certainly looks like it," I said, feeling rather put out. He returned to his paper. I stood looking at him. He lit a cigarette.

"Could you pass the ashtray?" Resisting a strong impulse to tip its contents over his shiny head, I banged it down on the table.

"Are you going to mop it up, or aren't you?" I said crossly.

"Oh. Ah. Well. Not now, at any rate." He was succeeding in making me determined to win this once and for all. I had an inspiration.

"It's taking the polish off the floor . . ."

It succeeded better than I could have dreamed. Muttering oaths directed towards all children ever created, he grabbed a bucket and a mop and leapt up the stairs – overcoming, no doubt with great fortitude, the anguish his old war wound must have been causing him. I followed more slowly, but triumphant. When I got back to the counter, Mr Tovey was looking rather bemused.

"How did you manage it?" I explained about the polish.

"Well done. It's quite an achievement to get him out of there before five-thirty."

Mr Stewart walked past, glowering. I glanced into the children's library, and saw the offending evidence still there.

"It's still there," I called, temporarily forgetting the silence rule.

"It bloody isn't," floated musically back to me, as Mr Stewart disappeared down the hall of pin-ups. Resisting the natural reply that it bloody was, I dragged him back and pointed to it.

"Well, that's another one then, because I mopped one up in non-fiction. Like ruddy cats and dogs it is." And he set to and removed that evidence too.

I was beginning to feel that this was an experience on the same level as the school-room phantom story, and that puddles were likely to spring up, or down, everywhere. I had to find the source. Where was the boy? I thought he had gone, but obviously not. I had to track him down, before the whole library was drowned. Perhaps by now he had found his mother, and they could both be persuaded to leave. I walked round the non-fiction, but there were no boys there. Equally, the children's library was now empty.

However in the fiction department there were still a number of people. Including the second lady I had spoken to. And a small boy, standing very close to her. She looked at me defiantly. I had no fight left. I went back to the counter.

"About time you went home," said Tovey. "Had enough, have you?" I had.

6

"Here Is Mr Okimbu"

I knew what to expect when I went in next morning. Tidy the books – fiction and non-fiction. This seemed to take a remarkably long time; much more than the hour and a half it actually was. But when it was finished, Tovey had a new delight in store. It stood there, quiet but menacing, in the corner; the switchboard. It had spent a lot of that first Monday morning groaning quietly to itself, and usually when there was no-one but me in the counter area.

It seemed an idiotic machine; as though it had life but no reason. It made a constant buzz once someone rang up, buzzing on and on until someone managed to find the time to answer it. And as well as buzzing, a metal tag about the size of a five pence piece would suddenly drop down, revealing a baleful eye, with the number 1, 2 or 3 on it, according to which line the call had come in on. And finally, a clip which held the 'eyelid' up until someone rang, moved senselessly up and down until the call was answered. In fact, if you can picture someone humming loudly, on one note, with one eye wide open and the eyebrow constantly moving up and down – you have a fair idea of the effect you produce when you telephone the local library.

"Now then Ken," said Tovey, "it's about time we started you off on the switchboard."

He led me over to the evil and confusing object, and we stood meekly in front of it, as though waiting for an audience.

"Now, these three eyes on the top left represent the three lines we have – 2293, 2294 and 2295. If someone rings up and 2293 is already engaged, they are auto-matically passed on to 2294. OK?"

That seemed simple enough. But it was only the preface. Here beginneth the first lesson.

"Now – when someone rings up, all you have to do is push up – or down – the key under the appropriate eye, and push up – or down – as long as it is the same – the key at the other end. Then you lift up your own phone, push the 'eyelid' back into place, and you're away."

"Why up – or down? Does it matter?"

"No – as long as they are both the same. You see, by moving them in the same direction you're connecting the two points – one to the incoming caller, one to your own phone. Now, as soon as someone rings, I'll let you try it."

For a while I served at the counter, awaiting the sound of doom. As people came and went I was beginning to feel quite pleased with myself. It seemed to be a lucky morning; I was having no trouble with the tickets at all. And even when Mr Tovey was called away and I was left alone in the counter, I seemed to be managing. Coping with both sides at once, I was; people returning books, people taking books out. Over to one side to find the tickets, back to the other stamping books out. Until the fateful moment when someone appeared at both sides of the counter at the same time. I thought I would go to the out counter first, as this was generally quicker and less likely to cause trouble. I should have known.

"Can I reserve two books please?"

"Oh – can you wait a moment?" I asked winningly. "I'll just give this lady her tickets and I'll be right back." I darted across the counter area, opened up the books, moved along the line of ticket trays and started flipping through the appropriate file. When, of course, it happened.

Bzzzzzzzzz, it went. It was, I thought, a most un-reasonable time to ring. I decided to leave it. Either Tovey would come back, or one of the other assistants would come to the rescue, or they would ring off. It seemed fair, after all, that those present should receive precedence over those ringing from home. And they could easily ring again. Bzzzzzzzzz, it went on, firmly. I set my jaw, and determined to ignore it. Bzzzzzzzzz, it continued, most insistently.

I looked across at it, witheringly. The lady I was serving looked at it. The lady wanting to reserve her books looked at it. Everybody seemed to be looking at it, other than those who could actually do something about it. Tovey was obdurately missing. Jill Shaw was languidly tidying her books and didn't even bother to look at first; when at last she did it was only with passing interest as she wandered round behind a bookcase and vanished. Bzzzzzzzzz it continued, happily.

"I'd better answer it," I said to my lady, and smiled. She smiled back. I went over to it, hoping I could remember what to do. I pushed the first key, and then the second; then pushed the eyelid up. I held the phone to my ear, and found the silence deafening.

"Central Library," I said rather diffidently, feeling I was barely qualified to represent it yet. But the silence continued.

"Central Library – hullo?" I tried again. The silence continued, as inexorably as the buzzing it had replaced.

"They've probably rung off," said Tovey, materializing suddenly. "Once the eye's dropped down – even if they hang up – it goes on buzzing till you shove the eye back up." So my first brush with the switchboard had resulted in a convincing win for it: Switchboard 1 (after extra time), Hornsby 0.

Tovey quickly disposed of the reserve-books lady; Jill so far forgot herself as to take over the lady coming in; and I was left to lick my wounds. Bzzzzzzzzz it suddenly went again. I was standing so near to it that its very closeness stunned me for a moment. Then I pulled myself together, went through the process of keys and eyes, and spoke:

"Central Library?"

"Ah – is that the library speaking?" Well, in a sense

it was. At least, part of it.

"Yes – Central Library here."

"I'd like to renew two books please. I have the numbers." It looked as though I was going to be lucky. An easy question, and an organized questioner.

"Right – can you give them to me please?" She started to read out, slowly and clearly, the two numbers. She was just starting the second when the switchboard struck again.

Bzzzzzzzzz it went– and a different eye, without a lid, and halfway along the board, blinked open. This was totally baffling. I'd never even seen this happen before, let alone had any idea what to do about it. And it was most unnerving. With my eyelid pushed up, but the noise still carrying on, it seemed an impossible, surrealist situation. Like closing the window because it was raining, and continuing to get wet. Furthermore, I couldn't even hear my caller.

"Are you still there? What is that terrible noise?" I half heard her shout. "Can you hear me? Is that the library speaking?" she went on.

Finally, just when I was deciding I might be well advised to give the city a second chance, Tovey appeared again, leaned across, pushed two different keys downwards, stopped the buzzing, and disappeared as silently as he had come.

"Sorry," I said to the telephone, "but something seemed to happen to the switchboard...." But the dead sound told me she had gone. Switchboard 2, Hornsby 0.

"What happened then?" I asked Tovey, who had appeared again, in rather a dispirited voice.

"Oh, that was Colin in Cataloguing. I just gave him a line." This I took, correctly, to mean switch a line through to him upstairs so he could dial straight out. But then a thought struck me.

"But how did you know he wanted a line?"

"Ah, well, he always rings his bookmaker about now." There was obviously a lot more to learn about being a telephone operator in a library than just operating the telephone.

One of these things was coping with Mr Okimbu. I'd been there about a fortnight when I first heard of Mr Okimbu. Jill was answering the phone, and I heard her say, "Can you hang on a moment, I'll get someone to deal with it for you." From this I supposed it was a matter of some importance, and that Tovey or Beaver were about to be involved. But no, Jill came up to me, and asked very nicely if I could look after some renewals on the phone, as she was rather caught up with something else at the moment. I couldn't see what exactly she was caught up with, but I didn't feel in much of a position to argue, so I approached the phone, pencil and paper in hand, ready to take down the numbers.

"Hullo . . ." I began, but was instantly stopped.

"Here is Mr Okimbu," boomed the phone, in a very dark brown voice.

"Right," I answered, waiting for Mr Okimbu to come to the phone and speak.

"Ready?" boomed the voice.

"Yes, put him on," I replied.

"Here *is* Mr Okimbu," it boomed again.

"Yes – right."

"You've got that?"

"Yes – if you'll put him on, I'll speak to him."

"Here *is* Mr Okimbu." I fell in at last. "Here is" meant in that dark brown language "I am".

"Right, Mr Okimbu, go ahead please. I'm all ready."

I was by now fairly used to the system of taking telephone renewals. All it entailed was taking down the numbers, asking for the dates they were due back, then removing the tickets from their appropriate trays and placing them in today's booked-out tray. There was only one difficulty: to check before renewing each one that someone hadn't already reserved it. If they had, that book couldn't be renewed, but had to be brought back. This whole operation took about three minutes a book; less if you were lucky.

Paper and pencil at the ready, I started to take down the numbers from Mr Okimbu. But I wasn't at all prepared for what was to follow. He read out no less than 23 books. After spilling from one piece of paper to a second, and then on to a third, I then had to ask the date on which they were due back.

"Yes indeed, but they are all different." I gulped. This was becoming a major production.

"Well, even so, I must have the dates. Can you read them out?" He had, of course, by now got the order completely muddled up, so that as he picked each book up at random, and read out the date due back, the order was quite different from mine. I was darting about desperately between my three pieces of paper, trying to match up numbers and dates, when he came to a sudden halt – when I reckoned he had three more to go. He was sure he had finished, so we had to go through the whole procedure again, before I got a date against every number. Finally I had them all down, and asked Mr Okimbu to wait. But the first ticket wasn't in its place; neither was the second; nor the third. And it soon occurred to me that all were wildly overdue anyway.

"Mr Okimbu . . . " I started rather hopelessly.

"Here is Mr Okimbu, thank you very much."

"Just a moment, please. I can't find the tickets under those dates; are you sure they are right?"

"They have been renewed before." This meant I had to start all over again.

"Oh, I see. Can you tell me when they were due back after you renewed them?"

"Yes indeed, but they are all different."

"Yes – but can you tell me when?"

"Either the twentieth or the twenty-eighth."

"And you don't know which?"

"No, I am very sorry indeed." By now it was quite obvious why Jill was 'caught up'. I was extremely caught up too. I started on the twentieth and the twenty-eighth. I found most of the tickets, and returned to the phone to ask about the others.

"Here is Mr Okimbu."

"Yes, Mr Okimbu, but some of them don't seem to have been renewed at all."

"That's right. The lady said I couldn't because they were reserved."

"But if they're reserved, you ought to bring them back."

"But I am studying, you see. They are all law books."

"But if someone else has reserved them, you must bring them back."

"But I need them for my studying."

"All you can do is reserve them for yourself, and when it's your turn, you will get them back."

"But I need them."

"Well, I'm sorry, but you can't renew them."

"OK." I renewed the others, told him the dates they were now due back, and rang thankfully off. Then two thoughts struck me. I hadn't checked whether the ones I *had* renewed were reserved. And secondly, wasn't there something a little too easy about that final "OK"? Yes, there was, I decided. It would be a long time before those books saw the library again, renewed or not renewed. It was, after all, a lot cheaper to pay a fine than buy the books outright.

After that performance, Beaver obviously took pity on me, and in a rare moment of irresponsibility, showed me a trick with the switchboard. By flicking a switch which stopped the buzzer ringing at all, and then by pushing *all* the top row of keys upwards at the same time, and then by flicking the buzzer switch down again momentarily – all the eyes, for internal and external lines, blinked at the same moment. A memorable, and indescribably agreeable, happening.

7

Bless the BNB

Walking about the library, going about your lawful business, you were an open and available invitation for any reader to ask you for help. Quite reasonable, really; you *were* there to help, one way or another. Unfortunately, helping was often more complicated than you could expect.

I soon learnt the basics; I already knew more or less how to use the catalogue (which I discovered a surprising number of people didn't). I soon learnt about the BNB – British National Bibliography – too. Unlike the catalogue, this was not available to the public, and was closely guarded by Colin of Cataloguing. The BNB represented the only way of discovering who the author was of any given book. And then once you had the author, it was easy to find out if we had the book in the library, simply by looking up his name in the public catalogue.

A perfect example of the system in action would be as follows. Ordinary reader to me: "Excuse me, I want to read a book called *The Wonderful Volunteer With Red Hair.* Is it here?" Me: "If you just like to wait, I'll find out." I then visit the BNB to find out the author. I then visit the catalogue, look up the author and discover we do (or don't) possess the book. I then visit the shelf where it should live. I then offer to reserve it for the reader, because it isn't there.

That is the system at its simplest, and working properly. But sometimes, what seems like a perfectly simple question can turn into a nightmare.

"Excuse me," said a light brown voice (cousin of Mr

Okimbu?) one extremely hectic Saturday. "I am looking for this book, you see, and I am not finding it. I am
wondering whether you can be helping me?" My heart
sank a little. No-one could call me racialist in any shape
or form, yet it was a fact that any question accompanied
by a brown voice always turned out to be complicated.
This was destined to be no exception.

"Yes?" I said warily.

"I am looking for *The CJ's.*"

"*The CJ's.*"

"Yes."

"Do you know who wrote it?"

"I'm afraid not."

"You're hoping I do?"

"Yes," he said, smiling in a winning way.

"What sort of book is it?"

"Indeed, it is a reading book."

"Yes, I'm sure it is, but for a start is it fiction or
non-fiction?"

"No, I don't think so. I think it is a novel."

That was something. It wasn't much, though, because
current novels were harder to trace. They came and
went at such a speed that they tended not to be so well
documented as non-fiction, which was altogether a more
stable breed of book. Anyway, it certainly meant a visit
upstairs.

"If you like to wait here a few minutes, I'll go and see
if we have it. OK?"

"OK. I will be waiting over here." I set off towards
cataloguing. On the way, I passed Mr Tovey.

"You don't know *The CJ's,* I suppose, do you?" I
asked, hoping with luck to short-circuit the whole
system.

"Sounds like an army regiment. Try Military Recollections."

"No, it's a novel."

"Never heard of it. S'pose the next thing is he'll be
bloody reserving it." (Tovey didn't like reservations; in
fact I never heard him use the word without 'bloody'

before it.) He wasn't really in a very jolly mood. He disliked Saturdays. We most of us disliked Saturdays. It was like working in a bargain basement, with everyone asking silly questions. I went upstairs.

I found the BNB, and looked up *The CJ's*. Not really to my surprise, I couldn't find it.

It being Saturday afternoon, Colin wasn't there to ask. In fact no-one was there to ask (they worked normal office hours in that department).

I stood still for a moment, trying to decide what I was doing wrong. It was, I was sure, much more likely to be me than the BNB that was at fault. But try as I might, I couldn't get it to give up its secret. *The CJ's* remained determinedly anonymous. Clearly I needed help.

It was no use asking Tovey, or anyone else downstairs, for help. They were far too busy. But with a sudden inspiration I remembered that at least one – and possibly both – of the ladies who ran the reference library were fully qualified, and thus very likely to be able to put me on the right track.

Cautiously, because it was a silent and unknown territory, I poked my head into the reference library, appearing silently at the back of the small counter area which served both as a desk for the reference librarian, and the entry and exit point for the public. It was the senior lady on duty.

"I'm sorry to bo. . . "

"Christ!" she said unexpectedly, jumping several inches, "whatever are you doing in there?" I explained the problem. Fortunately she didn't seem very busy; she nodded understandingly.

"Look," she said, "I can't leave the desk here – bring the BNB to me and I'll have a look." I may not have mentioned it, but the BNB was large and heavy and in several parts. I thought I had better take them all, in case my inexperience was causing me to look in the wrong one. I staggered back to the reference library, breathless with the weight.

She looked hard at the armful of books, and at me,

and smiled quietly and a little sadly. That was somehow worse than if she'd said, "You idiot, why did you bother to bring all those?" I set the books down, and she started to hunt, just like I had hunted. She found nothing, just like I had found nothing. She pursed her lips.

"*The CJ's,* you said?"

"*The CJ's.*"

"I wonder if it could be non-fiction. You could try Military Recollections." We both tried Military Recollections, but it wasn't there. She suddenly had a bright idea.

"Just a minute – I'll ring up David Ventnor at one of the branch libraries. He's got an encyclopaedic memory. I'll bet he knows." She rang him up, and he didn't.

"Well, I don't know," she said, looking baffled. "I'm sorry, I can't think of anything else. You'll just have to go and apologize. Or ask Mr Tovey." I staggered back with the BNB, and set off downstairs. On the way, I met the chief, who didn't usually work Saturday afternoons.

"Hello, Chiltern," he said cheerily. I didn't bother to attempt to put that right, but I did take the opportunity to ask him about *The CJ's.*

"Don't know," he said, "don't know anything on Saturday afternoons."

I had one last chance. I sought out Bill Davies, the man who the entire borough believed to be the chief librarian, and wasn't. He had been around a long time; he ought to know if anyone would.

"Do you know *The CJ's*"? I asked.

"What is it, a coffee bar?"

"No, it's a book – a novel, I think."

"Who wants it?"

"That man over there – the one with the green book in his hand."

"Why?"

I didn't feel this line of argument was getting me anywhere; I tried one last direct question.

"Have you heard of it?"

"No."

That was that. I couldn't think of anything else to try. I went rather crestfallen back into the lending library.

"I'm sorry . . . " I started. "Not to worrying," he said, light brownly. "I am finding the book in question is here after all on the shelf. See." And he held out the green book he was holding. The book that was causing all the trouble. The book that no-one had heard of. The book that no-one could find. I looked at it with regret and irritation. It was called *The Sea Chase.*

8

Loverly Tea

Going into the tea-room, I discovered, engendered a feeling rather like that experienced by a triumphant gladiator returning from the arena. The effect of a tyrannous public on a motley collection of library assistants cannot be dissimilar; the public are exhausting, belligerent, cantankerous, demanding, searching, realistic, hard work, and not to be put off. You enter the tea-room with the air of someone who has successfully fought several bulls and needs to get his breath back before he fights several more.

I quickly began to treasure tea breaks. For one thing, it was the only time when I met staff from other parts of the library. For instance, it took me four days before I ever met Colin of Cataloguing. When I did meet him, it turned out to be an entirely different battle of wits from that I experienced downstairs in the lending library. I might have guessed, I suppose, that the seats in the tea-room were like a railway commuters' carriage. Certain seats belonged to certain people, and it didn't do to choose the wrong one.

On my fourth day, I was at tea with Chiltern and Janet. They were sitting at the table, both writing. I didn't want to write, so I thought I'd take one of the three easy chairs. The one by the window looked inviting; it gave me a view of the high street I had never seen before, and it was in the sun. Still enjoying my gladiatorial feeling, I poured my tea and flopped down, beginning to feel a little at home. The door opened, and Colin came in.

I had never met him face to face; I had seen him in

the cataloguing department, and I was aware that at 10.15 he needed to have a line in order to ring his bookmaker. But apart from the fact that he bore a striking resemblance to a mouse, that was the sum total of my knowledge about him. His mousiness came from a basically furtive air, complemented by a long nose, a pointed chin, a broad moustache looking quite at odds with a thin face, and a general downward cast to his appearance. He was, I had learned, devoted to his job, which he did with meticulous care and attention.

Colin came in. I looked up, ready to show willing and be friendly. I smiled at him. He looked at me, and then at the seat I was in. He looked at Chiltern and Janet, who looked back interestedly, and then looked at me again. I sensed all was not well, but didn't know what. I felt he was not being as friendly as he might, given I was the new boy, but I was willing to give him the benefit of the doubt and accept that he was shy as well as mousy. I nodded towards the sunlight. "Nice, isn't it?" I said, tentatively.

"You can *see* the sun from there," he said meaningfully.

"That's so," I said, "that's certainly so. About the best seat in the room, this," I went on.

"That's right. It is."

I began to understand. I also began to be irritated. I had always felt the commuter seat argument to be a thin one, and I didn't feel this to be any stronger. I realized that being in charge of cataloguing was a senior position to that of an assistant librarian with slightly under four days' experience, but that didn't stop my being irritated. It was, I felt, a childish attitude for anyone to take about something so basically unimportant as a seat. But if you were a mouse as well as a child, the situation then looked thoroughly ridiculous. I thought I'd attack.

"Am I sitting in your favourite chair?" I asked, hoping to make the whole thing seem silly.

This simple move put Colin at an instant disadvantage. If he replied "No, of course not" (which any

self respecting cataloguer would) I had won for ever-
more. If he said "Yes, it is," he would inevitably make
himself look foolish, not to say grandfatherly. He
thought he'd try a little gamesmanship too.

"Well, it's the best seat in the room, so I suppose it's
everyone's favourite."

I looked across at Chiltern, who had not chosen
everyone's favourite seat. Chiltern had gone totally deaf
during the last three minutes, though he'd never shown
any signs of it before, and was determinedly ignoring the
whole thing.

I looked at Janet, who had also not chosen everyone's
favourite seat. She had recently found it necessary to
look very closely into the bag of sandwiches she had
before her on the table, in order to see I didn't understand what. Curiously, looking in the bag had made her
shoulders shake slightly. Colin was still standing looking
discomforted. Suddenly, I knew exactly what to do. I
stood up.

"You have it," I said submissively. Colin looked
mollified.

"It's time for me to go back," I added, as poor Janet
got a sudden coughing fit.

I went back, to face the marauding public again. But
that early brush with Colin had not been a typical
tea-break. They were usually much more pleasant. The
best ones were the half-hour breaks; on these occasions a
lot of people came together who did so at no other time.
One of the two reference librarians was usually there.
Both were middle-aged women, both rather intense,
both rather intellectual. Colin, plus an assistant of his,
plus the cataloguing clerk (whose job I never understood), plus Mr Tovey, plus Beaver or Chiltern or Janet
or Jill, would also be there for at least ten of the thirty
minutes. Bill Davies lived so close to the library he
would usually go home. The conversation was not, to say
the least, high-flown. It was also seldom to do with
librarianship. A typical scene might go as follows.

Colin (to Beaver): "It lost. That's the third this week."

Beaver (to the room at large): "Only the bookies win."

Reference librarian (to Janet): "Have you ever tried to grow hibiscus?"

Janet (to reference librarian): "I couldn't even spell it."

Tovey (to no-one in particular): "Bloody reservations."

No-one in particular (to Tovey): "You're right."

Janet (to Chiltern): "What's the number for tuberculosis?"

Chiltern (to Tovey): "What's the number for tuberculosis?"

Colin (to himself): "White Trout in the four-thirty."

Beaver (to himself, but loud enough for Colin to hear): "Mugs' game."

Janet (to Tovey and Chiltern): "Is it a five hundred?"

Tovey (to Janet): "If you want it, bloody reserve it yourself".

Chiltern (to Janet, looking at the reference librarian): "h – i – b – i – s – c – u – s."

Reference librarian (to Chiltern and Janet): "No, have you ever *grown* it?"

It really was just like family tea. If you had a rather large family. And didn't necessarily like tea.

9

Readers' Enquiries

One day, Tovey decided to rationalize the system of reader help. As I have said, every member of staff is a walking invitation to ask for help. And quite rightly. Yet it was also a fact that every member of the staff had other jobs to do – all of which were helping the public too, though rather less directly. For example, the girl walking about with a piece of paper in her hand, looking apparently at random on the shelves, was not wasting her time, nor dawdling about waiting to be spoken to. She was probably checking that the books which had been reserved the previous day were not, in fact, in their right places on the shelves all the time. Which at least a quarter of them were.

So Tovey decided he'd stop all the interruptions by creating a Readers' Enquiry Desk, and installing one of us there all the time. All questions anyone received in future were to be referred to this desk. Up to now there had been two people at work on the counter; one taking books in, one stamping them out. (Other than Saturdays, when it was a total free-for-all, all day.) So we now introduced a permanent third member, at a new desk built in to the counter, and marked 'Readers' Enquiries'. We were to take it in turns, in the normal forty-five minute stretches we did everything else in.

We started it one quiet Tuesday morning. To us, it was a radical departure. To the public at large, it was of no interest whatsover. We installed Chiltern as the first incumbent. Large, imposing, unshakeable, pompous, implacable, he sat there like an oracle, waiting to be consulted.

With astonishing single-mindedness, he was ignored by every member of the public who went past. But walking about putting my 900s away, someone accosted me.

"Can you tell me where I could find a book on Pekingese dogs?" asked a lady wearing what looked remarkably like a Pekingese dog around her neck. I was about to lead her off in the direction of the dog books, when I remembered the Readers' Enquiries desk.

"Would you just like to ask at the Readers' Enquiries desk?" I asked politely, and pointed towards the ponderous Jim Chiltern.

"Oh, in that case I won't bother," said the Pekingese dog collar, and wandered off.

It didn't seem quite the right attitude. Things didn't seem much better when I took up the position at the desk for the next turn myself. Nothing continued to happen. Then Jill Shaw, now on the incoming books side of the counter, suddenly realized she could get out of everything by simply sending them round to me.

"Can I renew my tickets?"

"Would you go round to the Enquiries desk?"

"Can I reserve *Lord of the Flies*?"

"Would you go round to the Enquiries desk?"

"Can I take this book out again?"

"Would you go round to the Enquiries desk?"

" 'Ere, love, 'ere's the post," said the postman appearing suddenly at the edge of the counter.

"Would you go round ... " started Jill, before she could get out of the habit.

I had imagined, before I joined the library, that the sort of queries we would get would be mildly intellectual. I wasn't sure how I was going to be able to help, but I was looking forward to the challenge. But the enquiries weren't much like that at all. And the provision of an Enquiries desk encouraged even more of the same. The following scene was typical.

Enter middle-aged lady, stage left, dressed in grey, with hat. She spies apparently idle young man, sitting vacantly at desk marked Readers' Enquiries. She thinks to herself "Aha," and approaches diffidently.

Lady: "Excuse me, young man, I wonder if you can help me?"

Me: "Yes madam?"

Lady: "I'm looking for a book."

Me (encouragingly): "Yes?"

Lady: "I want a love story."

Me: "A love story?"

Lady (now certain): "Yes."

Me: "Er . . . "

Lady: "Yes, I want a love story."

Me (looking at Jill for help, who steadfastly ignores my problem): "Have you tried the returned shelves?"

Lady: "Yes, I can't see anything there."

Me (stifling an urge to say "Well, put your glasses on then"): "Right, let's have a go."

(My remark didn't sound very suitable, I felt, but it matched my mood entirely. I knew little about love stories, and even less about what might suit this particular lady. 'Having a go' just about summed up the situation.)

I led her over to the returned shelves. I tried to think of suitable authors. Apart from Ruby M. Ayres, nothing sprang to mind.

"What about Barbara Cartland?" I said, with sudden inspiration. She sniffed, and I deduced Barbara Cartland was not to her taste. I looked at the dust jackets; a few seemed appropriate. I picked up one called *He Called Her Janie*.

"I brought that back," said the lady. I picked up *The Enraptured Isle*.

"I brought *that* back," said the lady. I picked up *The Love Machine*.

"I wouldn't read that," said the lady. I picked up *Dream of Susan*.

"I've read it," said the lady.

The situation was becoming desperate. There were two other people now waiting at my desk. Something had to be done.

"Just a moment," I said, as though I had had a sudden inspiration.

I went back into the counter to see what had arrived in the last few minutes, and found a book called *Love In The Nest*. Proudly I bore it out.

"Do you know this one?" I asked.

"No, I don't think I have . . . "

"Then take it; I'm sure you'll enjoy it."

"Do you recommend it?"

"I do." I had to; I couldn't think of anything else.

"Right," she said, "I will."

I handed it to Janet, who booked it out rapidly. The lady went happily. Janet giggled at me.

"Do you know what that was?" she asked.

"Presumably it was a slushy novel."

"Not at all. Didn't you notice it had a non-fiction number?" No. I hadn't.

"It was an ornithological book," Janet went on, chortling, "on the mating habits of the cuckoo."

The real test of the Readers' Enquiry desk came, however, on the first Saturday. Saturdays were, as I have said, something of a free-for-all. We gave up our individual jobs entirely – and apart from doing as much shelving as we could early in the day, we concentrated on the counter. For the first hour or so, it was reasonably quiet. One assistant took books in, one stamped them out, one sat, for the first time, at the Readers' Enquiry desk.

Everyone else was shelving, with the exception of Tovey, in the office, and Bill Davies – the curl of smoke over the stockroom telling where he was. Throughout the week, the new system had worked tolerably well; but then it had been under no real strain. If occasionally one of the three in the counter had been overloaded, one of the others would help out. In particular, the enquiries man would lend a bit of weight when needed; he was specially useful with the telephone. But Saturday had never been the same as a weekday, and we should have known better than to expect it all to go smoothly.

Tovey had decided that now we had the luxury of an extra hand on the counter, he didn't need to keep such a continuous eye on it. So when things started to go wrong, he wasn't there to backstop it. The cast was as follows: Beaver was at the enquiry desk, Chiltern receiving books, and I sending them out.

The first sign of trouble was the appearance of an old and gnarled hand around the nearest edge of the counter to the front door. I had noticed this ploy before. Despite the fact that the owner of the hand had presumably left her own home, walked along the high street to the library, got up the steps, through the foyer, and across the hall to the counter, she managed to give the impression that there was no chance in the world that she could go any further. It meant, in other words, she needed someone to manage the entire library process for her: receive her books, check them in, hang on to the tickets, find suitable books, check them out, hand them back to her. Meanwhile, the old and gnarled hand would continue to grace the edge of the counter, as a constant reminder that age comes to us all; that we should thank our lucky stars it hasn't struck yet; and that we should treat her with respect and help.

"Aha," thought Chiltern, on the receiving end, "this is a job for reader enquiry Beaver."

"Mr Beaver," he hissed, "give us a hand." Beaver, in one of his rare moments of humour, looked pointedly at the presence on the edge of the counter, and replied, "You've already got one." Chiltern, who knew not only when and how to be deaf, but also when and how to ignore humour when it meant "I won't," said loudly to the hand. "Would you please go round to the Readers' Enquiry desk?"

"It's my foot," said the hand.

Even Chiltern couldn't fail to see the unintentional humour in that one. Despite himself, he gave in and went so far as to accept the returned books. Then he said to Beaver, "Look, I've taken them in, here are the tickets, I've got a queue of people waiting with more books – can you find her two light novels?" Beaver realized he had no option and disappeared towards the answer for most problems – the returned book shelves – and vanished into a mass of people.

The hand remained where it was, causing a complicated wriggle to the shape of the queue of incoming readers. At this moment, Mrs Bell (without Susan) suddenly appeared at the enquiry desk – which was, of course, now unmanned.

"Ah," she boomed, "what an excellent idea. An enquiry desk."

As Chiltern was surrounded by a queue, and haunted by a hand, and as Beaver was away looking for two light novels, that left me. At that precise moment, no-one was going out, so I felt I had no reason not to notice and reply.

"Yes," I said brightly, wandering across to her. "It's new – just started this week. It seems to be working quite well."

"Well," echoed Mrs Bell, "let me take full advantage of it." And she started fishing in her handbag. Two warning bells sounded in my mind.

One: when women fished in their handbags it nearly always meant one thing – they were looking for a list of books they had always wanted. Needless to say, either we didn't have the books, or they weren't in (which meant a bloody reservation).

Two: Mrs Bell hadn't realized that there should have been someone seated there; instead she had presumed that anyone within the counter whom she could attract would do. I was nearby; she had attracted me; and now she expected help. Unfortunately I wasn't supposed to be there. "Now I've got this list . . . " she began. At this moment, a young couple appeared at the check-out, books in hands.

"I must just go and stamp those books," I said hopefully, easing myself away.

"Indeed you won't," retorted Mrs Bell, resorting to full dignity at the prospect of losing her newly found aide.

"You are providing a reader advisory service," she went on, "and I wish to be advised."

"But I'm not actually the person who . . . "

"Don't start that job demarcation business with me, young man, or I shall ask to see Mr Mortimore. Please help me find these books." I felt singularly helpless. Beaver hadn't returned; Chiltern still had his queue, and his hand. Tovey was nowhere to be seen. The curl of smoke continued uninterrupted from the stockroom. Neither of the girls was in sight.

I didn't seem to have any option. Hoping the young couple would be more interested in themselves than in the failure of the borough library service to allow them to leave its central library, I took Mrs Bell's list in my hand and set off towards the catalogue, with her trailing behind me. At that moment, the phone began to buzz.

Even Mrs Bell could understand that I couldn't ignore that. I apologized to her and returned to the switch-board. At that moment Beaver came back with books for the hand, and seeing me on the phone, proceeded to stamp them, and then dealt with the young couple. The phone turned out to be a wrong number, and I turned to Mrs Bell again. By then the queue, and the hand, had gone, but a new queue had formed at the enquiry desk.

Beaver was by now fully occupied at the out counter, and I was out in the library itself, attending to Mrs Bell. Chiltern had no option but to become reader enquiry agent. Mr Tovey then appeared, looking baffled. And well he might: the reader enquiry man was checking books out; the book checker-out was missing, presumed being a reader enquiry man; the book checker-in was also being a reader enquiry man. There was no-one checking books in; Mr Tovey then became book checker-in. Then the phone rang. I rushed back and answered it. Choosing its moment with extreme care, it said, dark brownly, "Here is Mr Okimbu." I looked at Jill Shaw, who had carelessly walked into view. And I looked at my conscience. My conscience lost. Holding out the phone to her I said, "It's for you."

10

Reckoning with the Reading Room

An important element in the library, if not the most serious, was the reading room. As a title, reading room was something of a misnomer. The sleeper, or the relaxer, or the keep-out-of-the-rainer, might be more appropriate. It was a difficult room to deal with, because you didn't need to be a member of the library to use it, and no-one could ever prove you weren't using it properly. It was over-run by tramps at nine-thirty, by charladies at eleven, by children at four-thirty, and by everyone when it was raining or there had been a disaster. All the daily papers were to be found there, neatly attached each one to a reading board rather like a lectern. The most popular weekly and monthly periodicals were there too – although what constituted 'popular' was a matter for constant discussion.

Looking after it was a job everyone wanted in some respects, and everyone hated in others. It was understandable, when you thought about it, that Jill liked being in charge of it best. It gave her the perfect excuse, whenever the phone buzzed, or a difficult customer loomed on the horizon, or there were a lot of reservations, to say "I must just go and tidy the reading room," and she had the perfect reason for leaving it all behind her. Once there it could easily be half-an-hour before she reappeared.

I once followed her in to see what she did. It was a revelation. She went in. And she sat down in front of a magazine. Twenty minutes later she got up. And came out.

The reading room was also where Grape-nuts lived. I first met Grape-nuts in my second week.

"Go and have a look at the reading room," said Tovey, "the *Children's Newspaper*'s gone missing again. It's probably in there somewhere." I went in, and came out almost immediately.

"Mr Tovey – something horrible's happened in there. I don't know whether it's a dead cat, or a child being sick, or the drains, but there's the most appalling smell."

"Ah," said Tovey knowledgeably, "does it smell like week-old cabbage?"

"Exactly," I said, feeling somewhat relieved because Tovey knew what it was.

"Grape-nuts," said Tovey.

"Sorry?" I enquired.

"Grape-nuts. Man eating grape-nuts. Throw him out." I looked at Tovey rather uncertainly. Janet grinned and nodded. Jill muttered "Oh God," and disappeared. Chiltern had a brief but serious attack of deafness. I went back. The smell was overpowering. I looked round, and just as Tovey had said, there was a tramp eating grape-nuts – and equally as Tovey had suggested, he was the root of the smell.

I hadn't reckoned, when I wrote my famous letter to the chief about following suitable courses and progressing up the ladder, that I was likely to be employed in the role of defumigator/policeman too. However, I assumed I was a little higher up the social scale than the tramp – if only because I was working there – so adopting a fairly lofty voice I said, "Come along now, out you go." Grape-nuts stood up to a surprising height, and amid the sudden silence said in a voice straight from Eton,

"I beg your pardon young man, but would you like to describe to me exactly upon what grounds you wish me to vacate these premises?" You won't be particularly surprised to learn I was speechless. Well, nearly.

"Ahhhhum," I replied cautiously, "are you a member of this library?"

"As you must know, young man, as presumably you

68

are employed by the borough to serve in this establish-
ment, it is no part of the borough's requirements that I
should be a registered member of the lending library in
order to partake of its facilities in respect of the newspaper reading room."

Subduing the over-riding impulse to reply, "It undoubtedly should be part of the requirements that you
refrain from smelling like Old Nick's boots," I beat a
feeble retreat to ask for enlightenment from Tovey.

"He wasn't quite what I expected . . ." I began,
hopelessly.

"Difficult case, Grape-nuts," said Tovey. "He's a
doctor, you know. The National Health Service drove
him mad. Literally. He won't deal with National Health
patients, and – not surprisingly – private patients won't
deal with him. So he lives on grape-nuts and saves a lot
on water and soap. Chiltern – throw him out." I felt
rather put out myself at being quite so inadequate and
hoped rather sulkily that Chiltern hadn't yet recovered
from his attack of deafness. Rather to my surprise however, he nodded quite amiably, and disappeared into the
reading room. Seconds later, Grape-nuts appeared and
scuttled out.

"Whatever did you say?" I asked.

"Told him we'd call the Borough Health Inspector,"
said Chiltern. "It always works."

"Nothing but bloody trouble, that reading room,"
said Tovey. "That, and bloody reservations."

Despite the noticeable and lasting effect of Grapenuts,
and the somewhat illiterate nature of the inhabitants, I
felt the reading room had an interesting atmosphere. It
was part of the library, and yet it wasn't. Its purpose was
similar, yet the feeling in the room was quite different. It
also had its own organizational problems, as I was to
find out.

"Ken – next week, the reading room," announced
Beaver one Friday. I was still not above enjoying a little
verbal fencing with Beaver.

"Next week the reading room what?" I asked blank-faced. He also could play games.

"Next week the reading room has you looking after it," he squeaked, equally blank-faced.

I had lost that one. "What do I have to do?" I asked.

"Put the papers in first thing in the morning, pop in throughout the day to keep an eye on it and tidy up a bit, and take the papers out in the evening. Nothing to it."

So the next Monday morning I collected the newspapers from Mr Stewart the janitor, and marched in with them. My public was already waiting. That is to say a very old man was standing in the corner, trying to disguise the fact that he had an extremely evil pipe thoroughly alight behind his hand, and an equally old lady was spread-eagled over two chairs in the other corner, recovering from her early morning cleaning stint in a local office block. Seeing me arrive, the room began rapidly to fill with other regulars. I put the papers down on the big table, sorted out the *Daily Telegraph*, which seemed a reasonable place to begin, found its lectern, and began to fix it in. It all seemed neat and satisfactory. I got a small pleasure from the tidy way in which the paper slipped into its place beneath the brass holder, and sat there, clean and bright, waiting for its first reader. I turned back to the table for the next paper.

Immediately I realized things were not quite so neat and organized as I had believed. My public had seized the papers the minute my back was turned, and not one was left. In fact, two of them were not even left in the building, but to be seen disappearing down the front steps with two of my faithful readers. I bounded after them, taking a leaf out of Beaver's book. They had, of course, gone in opposite directions so I was certain to lose one. Curiously, the choice was between *The Times* and the *Daily Mirror*. It didn't take me long to decide. *The Times* must be preserved at all costs. I shot after a man who would pass anytime for Grape-nuts's under-study, shouting "Let me have that paper back . . . you can't take that . . . it belongs to the library."

The understudy looked slightly sheepish and muttered something about not realizing, and handed me back the paper. I returned triumphantly with it, confirming as I did that I had lost the *Mirror* for good.

By the time I got back into the reading room, of course, any semblance of calm and order had completely disappeared. Instead of each of the papers being stuck firmly in its place, with person or persons standing patiently before it, they were everywhere.

All the papers had come apart; different people were reading different sections everywhere; some bits had been trampled underfoot. It was a daunting prospect. I took the manly decision, and realized it was impossible to bring order bit by bit, so I simply went around collecting every inch of newspaper I could find. I disregarded opposition of every sort, said a curt "Sorry," to everyone who remonstrated, and carried the whole lot off to the safety of the office.

Painstakingly I put each paper together again, applied liberal quantities of Sellotape, and then with them all firmly beneath my arm I returned and installed one at a time in their places, to the cool and sullen accompaniment of twenty pairs of eyes who had had their fun removed. When I had finished, it all looked pretty normal. With the exception of the one *Daily Mirror* lectern, which stared blankly at me with a reproving look on its face. With one accord, twenty pairs of eyes turned to look at me. Forty eyebrows were raised. One voice was heard to come from the table in the middle.

"Where's the bleeding *Mirror* then?" I looked back steadily.

"It's gone down the bleeding street, as you very well know," I said, and marched out, leaving the reading room quieter than it had ever been in its life.

.

11

Wednesday Afternoons

On Wednesday afternoons, the library was closed. I had known this for years, because it was always Wednesday afternoon when I finished whatever I had been reading and wanted to change it. When I came to work at the library, I had assumed that Wednesday would be the half day, to compensate for Saturday. Not a bit of it; Wednesday was a full day just like any other. It was just that the public weren't there.

This had a number of effects; the most obvious one (leaving aside the fact that we didn't have any customers) was the way everyone walked around smoking. Bill Davies's curl of smoke appeared everywhere. Tovey had a permanent cigarette drooping from his lips. Even Beaver, so controlled, permitted himself a cigarette from time to time (though he did carry an ashtray around with him all the time too). Neither of the girls smoked, and I sometimes smoked a pipe – though so infrequently I felt rather embarrassed whenever I did. Because, when I did, someone always said, "Oh, I didn't know you smoked. I like a pipe."

However, on my first Wednesday afternoon, I had no idea what to expect. I hadn't worked at all in the morning; my hours were the 'long afternoon' – one to eight-fifteen. I arrived at one to find I was the only one working those particular hours. Thus everyone else was at lunch for my first hour.

"What shall I do?" I asked Tovey, who was on all day (eight-forty-five to eight-fifteen – on the face of it a terrible stint, but Tovey was no fool, and knew what Wednesday afternoon meant).

"I should start with some shelving," he replied, unconsciously echoing Beaver's first remarks to me. I started. By two I was beginning to have had enough of it. Fortunately someone was presumably about to appear, and I could then do something more interesting. However, no-one did appear, other than an old lady wanting some love stories. She found it extremely difficult to understand why if I was there she couldn't have any.

I pointed to the notice displaying the opening hours, and also drew her attention to the wooden notice board on a stand that she had pushed out of the way in order to get to the counter. All that had no effect. I was there, wasn't I? So couldn't I just this once provide her with perhaps just one love book? She had no-one at home; her husband had died years ago; and her cat wasn't very well. Also she couldn't really see the television.

I didn't feel it would be very sporting of me to ask how, if she couldn't see the television, she expected to be able to see the words in a book. After some further discussion, i.e., she spoke and I listened, I decided it might be to everyone's advantage if I gave in. I took her two books in, and met the first difficulty. They were both overdue. That didn't matter in itself, except that the accounts for the day had been made up, so I couldn't put the fine money anywhere. This made it surprisingly difficult. I could hardly let her off, just because she had insisted on being attended to when we weren't open. Anyway, I felt I was making quite enough of a gesture in dealing with her at all. I could quite imagine what sort of change she'd have got out of Jill Shaw. There was no-one to ask, so finally I decided to take the money, put it in my pocket, and hope to be able to cook tomorrow's books somehow.

Having come to this decision, I asked for the money. What for, she asked? Because the books were overdue, I replied. But they couldn't be, she said. Because she had only taken them out last Wednesday afternoon. That was a false move, I thought. Last Wednesday afternoon, like this Wednesday afternoon, we were closed. I looked

73

hard at the date stamp, and showed her that it had in fact been three weeks ago last Thursday. Could I have the money, I asked again.

"Oh, I don't pay fines," she said. I was beginning to get a little exasperated.

"Why ever not?"

"Because I'm an old age pensioner," she explained triumphantly, "here's my pension book."

She produced a dog-eared buff-coloured book, and I was just inspecting it when Tovey came down the stairs, complete with drooping cigarette.

"Oh no, Mrs Beckwith, not again," he said. "I've told you more times than I can remember, we're not open on Wednesday afternoons. Now, run along." A number of thoughts struck me simultaneously. For one, wasn't it odd how we used the same terminology to the old as to the young? It must have been twenty years since Mrs Beckwith had run along anywhere. For another, I was looking pretty silly. Not to say caught red-handed bending the rules. For a third, she had been exploiting me shamelessly, and that riled. I assumed she was at least a little deaf, and echoed Tovey's words to my own satisfaction.

"Yes, come along Mrs Beckwith, run along," I said.

"Don't you talk to me like that, Mr er . . . Did you hear what he said, Mr Tovey?"

The fact that by uttering his name she revealed that she knew a lot more about the library than she had admitted to hardly helped her case, I thought.

"Yes, and he's quite right, Mrs Beckwith. Off you go now," said Tovey to my surprise. Grumbling, she departed.

"Ruddy bleeders," observed Tovey.

I couldn't make up my mind whether he had intended that remark just like it came out, or whether it was an unconscious Spoonerism for "bloody readers". Either way, it seemed a splendid phrase to me, and I adopted it forthwith.

Having despatched Mrs Beckwith, Tovey then proceeded to despatch me to the stockroom. I settled down at a table facing a frosted glass window, which gave straight out onto the street. I was lost in a new book about the Far East (not strictly what I was supposed to be doing) when I was rudely awakened by a sudden, rather furtive, knocking on the window. I knew that outside were seats where old men and old women and old dogs would slumber quietly in the summer sun – and I decided this was simply one of the more eccentric of these (although probably not one of the dogs). So I ignored it. But it happened again. Possibly one of the old men hoping to persuade me to let him borrow one of our under-the-counter books, like *Ulysses* (which I didn't feel he'd get a great deal out of), or *The Second Sex* (which I thought he might). Ignore it and it'll go away, I said to myself. So I did, and it didn't. I opened the window.

"Yes?" I enquired, coldly.

"Gross," said a man in overalls.

"Gross?"

"Gross. Binders. Come along mate." I was feeling a bit impatient by now.

"What do you mean, 'Gross, binders, come along mate'?"

"Gross. Binders," he repeated, much more loudly, but not at all more explanatorily.

"Wait a minute . . ." I said, puzzled.

"What for – bleedin' Christmas? You can have 'em now."

"There's a man at the window who insists on saying 'Gross, binders' to me. What's he on about?"

"Oh, he's from Gross. Binders."

From my expression, which was intended to tell him he wasn't actually adding much to my store of information, he realized that wasn't enough.

"The bookbinding company. Probably returning some books. Can you see to it for me?" asked Tovey with a kindly smile on his face; a smile which I read to mean "You've obviously got enough sense to stand in for me on occasions – and this is one of the occasions".

"Right," I said to the man outside the window, "what can I do for you?"

"I should ruddy 'ope so. 'Aven't got all day. 'Ere-yar." And with that he threw a large and heavy carton of books towards me through the window across the table.

"Thanks," I said, starting to close the window.

" 'Ang about, there's some more. You'd better move that," he said, pointing to the first carton. I lifted it up slowly, and dropped it quickly.

As he brought another, and another, and another, I began to appreciate what Tovey's smile had really said. It had said "You're being had for a sucker!" It said it very politely. But it definitely said it.

12

Those Quiet Evenings

Towards the end of the day – about seven in the evening
– we stopped behind-the-scenes work, and converged on
the counter. By that time there were usually only three
or four of us left, and the atmosphere became more
relaxed. Things seemed always to get on a more personal
level in the evening. Like the time a pretty young
housewife came in with four technical books under her
arm, all several weeks overdue. Despite the fact that they
have to pay fines, people are nearly always apologetic
when books are late. She was no exception.

"I'm really terribly sorry about this. I know they are at
least six weeks overdue. I don't really know what to say.
They are my husband's books, you see, and of course I've
got to bring them back for him." She looked me straight
in the face, with an honest, make-a-clean-breast-of-it
look.

"You know where they were, don't you?" she went on,
sadly. I didn't, and made a face to say so.

" . . . in his other home." She looked down in some
distress. I hardly knew what to say. Things like "Well, it
could happen to anyone," seemed hardly adequate for
the situation. "Oh, my goodness me," combined with a
hearty noncomprehending laugh might have got me out
of it. But she had looked me too straight in the eye, and
was too openly nice, for me to have pretended not to
have understood.

But what *do* you say when a pretty wife has just
admitted to you that her husband has another home,
and presumably another woman to go with it? In the
end I attempted one of those faces which said at one and

the same time "How sad/how unfortunate/I under-
stand/I won't comment/I'm sure he's the one in the
wrong/we must behave in a grown-up fashion/I don't
know what the world is coming to/he must be out of his
mind."

". . . in his other home," she repeated, "his *car*. He
seems to spend half his life in that car. Still, I suppose it's
not so surprising really. He's a rep, you know."

Free and easy was the best way to describe most
evenings. Occasionally, from Tovey's point of view, too
free and easy. Take Mr Tibbett. Mr Tibbett was one of
those readers whom I knew by sight, but not by name.
He was very knowledgeable about the library, about its
inhabitants (the staff), and his rights. At least, he
thought he was. One night he came in with six books,
and wanted to take out eight.

"I'm sorry, but if you only have six tickets, you can
only take out six books," I said politely.

"No," he said firmly, "you can take out as many as
you like. Would you please issue me with two extra
tickets."

"I can't do that, I'm afraid," I said, "the rules say six
tickets per person, and you've already got your six.
Unless you have a wife, or some grown-up children to
enrol, I cannot issue any more adult library tickets." I
was right, and within my rights, and I knew it. Mr
Tibbett either didn't know it, or didn't want to know it.

Tovey's ears had pricked up at the sound of the
altercation, and he wandered across to lend a little
weight to the proceedings. He put on his special 'senior'
voice; a tone that brooked no disagreement and appeared utterly final.

"He's right, you know. Six tickets a person it is."

Mr Tibbett, on his side, had signally failed to recognize the authority in Tovey's voice, and was afraid he
was going to have to insist on speaking to the chief
librarian. Tovey was on safe ground here, and smiled in
a relaxed way.

"I'm afraid you can't do that, Mr Tibbett, you'll have to make do with me. The chief doesn't work in the evenings; I'm in charge tonight."

"Nonsense," said Mr Tibbett, "I've seen him over there." He pointed in the direction of the stockroom. Tovey looked a little less happy.

It was possible that the chief had come in to choose a book or two for himself. His house was right next door, and he had a private door in through the children's library. Tovey was looking unhappy because, though without question we were right, it was not unknown for the chief to decide to 'make an exception' if the going got rough. And Tovey didn't want to lose face.

"I think you're mistaken," said Tovey, "but I'll go and have a look – although he'll say the same thing we did." Tovey went off, and I busied myself with nothing of any importance until Tovey returned.

He came back quickly and said he thought Mr Tibbett must have been mistaken, because the chief librarian certainly wasn't in tonight.

"This is nonsense," said Mr Tibbett again, "I shall find him myself."

Before we could stop him he strode off in the direction of the stockroom. Shamelessly ignoring the 'Private' sign, he marched in – closely followed by Mr Tovey and me.

"There," said Mr Tibbett triumphantly. "I wish to make a formal complaint. And furthermore, I wish to insist on being allowed to take an extra two books out with me tonight."

A look of extreme irritation spread over Tovey's face, contrasting strongly with the look of pleasure on Mr Tibbett's. He had succeeded, in spite of all opposition, in taking his case to the highest authority. For there, desperately looking for somewhere to stuff his smoking pipe, in the corner of the stockroom cowered Bill Davies. Mr Tovey's 'boss'. Looking at Tovey and Bill together, it was a mistake anyone could have made, I thought. The trouble was, from Tovey's point of view, most people did.

13

Hamster Havoc

One day, when Tovey was sitting in his office, doing nothing in particular extremely busily, and I was in there too, taking a healthy interest in *Modern Contraception*, Mr Mortimore walked in. This was an event in itself. It was almost the first time I could remember it happening. The chief came straight up to me.

"Beaver, send Mr Tovey to me, would you?" he said, and walked straight out again. Even for him, this was going a bit far. I had been there for about seven months by now, and he must have been able to tell us apart. And even aside from that, Tovey himself was only a matter of feet away. I looked at him.

"Blind as a bloody bat," he observed with a sigh. "Don't think he's read a book for bloody years." Tovey disappeared upstairs in the direction of the chief's office. Within five minutes, he was back.

"How would you like to go out on a branch?" he asked. This seemed one of the stranger suggestions put to me since I had joined the library service, and I said so.

"No, no, it means go on a branch visit. Help out at one of the branch libraries. Sickness has struck."

It seemed quite an interesting idea. I would be able to put my recently acquired knowledge to new use. And be able to flaunt my central library sophistication in one of the more provincial of our outlying buildings (all of three miles away). Accordingly I persuaded my old car to drive me the three miles to the branch, entered, and had a shock. The local chief was my friend Hugh; I had for some inexplicable reason not remembered that this was the branch he had taken over. So having avoided it

80

for seven months, I was suddenly working for him. Not that it seemed to matter. I soon discovered that there was a very different atmosphere out here; everything more relaxed, more informal.

I found the whole operation fascinating; the numbering system was, of course, the same, so I could very quickly find my way around, despite the fact that I had never been there in my life. It was a little uncanny in a way. I set about some shelving. There were, naturally, fewer books. There were also fewer staff, so I didn't feel I had gained much. But the air of informality showed up almost immediately.

As I stood by the returned books, engaged in the octopus fight, in came a man with a large brown paper parcel, roughly tied up with string and Sellotape. Having noticed him, I promptly forgot him, other than vaguely realizing out of the corner of my eye that he had gone to the back of the non-fiction department.

After a while, though, the sound of rustling began to impinge on my consciousness, and I realized it was coming from his direction. I walked quietly towards it, and found to my astonishment that he had undone his parcel, and taken out the Flying Scotsman. Or to be more precise, he had taken out a half-finished model of the Flying Scotsman. He was on his hands and knees, comparing it with several books he had out on the floor. Speechless, I stood and looked at him. He looked up.

"Hello," he said happily, and continued his examination. I went on feeling speechless. Or nearly.

"I don't think you should really be doing that," I said weakly.

"Oh, Hugh doesn't mind," he said, without even looking up. I went over to Hugh.

"There's a chap over there building a replica of the Flying Scotsman," I said, "he's got it all over the floor, and about half a dozen books spread everywhere . . . "

"Oh, good," said Hugh, "excellent." And shot off in the direction of the Flying Scotsman. I puffed after him. When I drew up, Hugh had his coat off, and was on the floor too. Working in a branch was clearly a lot removed from what I was used to – or had expected.

It was only a matter of minutes before the next surprise burst upon me; to be fair, it took Hugh by surprise too. The first intimation of excitement in store was a wild female shriek.

"Ooooh!" it went. And "Help!" it went. And "Go away you horrible thing!" it went.

Thinking that the unthinkable had happened, and that one of our female readers was being raped in the fiction, I hurtled off in the direction of the noise, to find a lady of about forty sitting at the top of the library step-ladder. At the bottom were two small boys, looking sorrowful and worried.

"Whatever's going on?" I demanded.

"We've lost Harry," one of them replied.

"Harry?"

"Yes, our hamster."

"Horrid ghastly rat thing," said the woman, "it went for my foot."

"They don't go for foots," said the boy, ungrammatically.

"It went for my foot," repeated the woman determinedly. "You've got to find it before we all get rabies."

I didn't feel this was the moment to stop and inform her she had a wild misunderstanding of nature if she thought that hamsters called Harry automatically carried rabies, but I did agree we ought to find it.

"Hugh," I shouted out, deciding to ignore the silence rule in the emergency, "we've lost a hamster." This was, almost certainly, the last thing I should have done. The information caused immediate chaos among all the other female readers in the library. Women started running everywhere. I remembered a line from one of my favourite authors: "he rushed off in all directions". It had always tickled me. The two boys were rushing around, calling "Harry", for all they were worth. The first woman was still sitting on the top of the steps, waving her legs around – for no good reason I could think of. Two other women jumped up backwards onto the counter, and also sat swinging their legs. Hugh appeared slowly, clearly much more interested in the Flying Scotsman. The other assistant, a silent girl of about seventeen, went mildly pale, stood transfixed to the spot, stared about hopelessly, and remained silent. Suddenly, nothing was happening. I felt the need to speak.

"Where is it?" I cried.

The sheer absurdity of my remark struck everyone simultaneously. A maniacal cackle from Hugh told me precisely how absurd it was, and he suggested, rather pointedly, that we might consider looking.

"Let us get in a row, and move along the library together," he said, taking charge magnificently.

Several men in the library joined us, together with one tough old lady in ankle boots who was determined not to be numbered among the weaker sex. In one long sweep, we started up the library. Silence. We crept stealthily on.

"There it is," called an old man.

We all swooped, triumphantly, on a dusty book which had fallen down behind some shelves. We set off again, vigilant as ever.

"There it is."

"No, it's gone."

"No, it's there, behind the A–Fs."

"It's a newspaper, you fool."

"No, it's *it.*"

"It is not an *it*," said one of the boys, hurt.

We surrounded the A–Fs. Sure enough, there was a very small hamster, washing its face.

"Come and get it," I called to the boys, using what was not perhaps the most appropriate phrase.

The boys appeared, one from each side. One had a bag. They got closer. Still it washed. They got closer still. It stopped washing. They stopped moving. It started washing again. The boy dropped the bag, very neatly, just after the hamster had shot off again, in the direction of the counter.

"Sod," said one boy carelessly.

"Don't let it out," shouted the other.

"It hasn't been date-stamped," called Hugh irreverently.

"It's coming your way; don't let it past," I called to the two ladies sitting on the counter. One of them squealed and slipped back against the switchboard, which promptly started to buzz.

"Answer it," said Hugh to the lady, "it's probably a rat-catcher."

I was seeing Hugh with new eyes. He may not have had the appropriate dignity to be a sober chief librarian, but he clearly had a great future as ringmaster in a circus.

"Tally ho," he shouted, and galloped towards the counter.

The lady who had slipped against the switchboard recoiled violently and jumped up again, as she thought, back onto the counter top. Unfortunately, what she actually landed on was the book trolley, which immediately took off at speed towards the non-fiction, the woman clinging on for dear life. The hamster suddenly decided not to leave, and instead sat down for tea, bulging its cheeks with the pages of a book which had landed on the floor amid all the confusion. I noticed, with passing interest, that the book was called *Food Storage*.

The boys encircled the hamster again, and were just about to drop the bag over it when a four letter word that tended to begin with 's' rang out around the library as the lady on the trolley rode triumphantly straight through the Flying Scotsman. The hamster took full advantage of this latest uproar to shoot away from the boys, and head unswervingly for the lady in ankle boots.

This full-frontal attack was suddenly too much for her, and she sat abruptly down on the floor, whereupon the hamster shot straight up her skirt. She let out the most astounded squawk of horror, and struggled to her feet. To the amazement of the entire audience, the hamster didn't reappear. We stood stock still in fascinated silence, not daring to think what might happen next, or indeed what was happening then. After what seemed like three and a half weeks, it suddenly landed at her feet, rolled over in a slight daze, and started washing again. With an inspired pincer movement, she brought her ankle boots together, and trapped it.

Hugh deemed this to be the moment when he should assert himself again, and rushed forward and bent down to pick it up. Whereupon it promptly bit him. Hugh jumped back swearing; the lady stepped away dazed; and the hamster hurtled off again.

By this time one or two other people had entered the library. There was no-one at the counter to let them in, so they stood stupefied watching the whole farce. One of them started cheering quietly.

Hugh was wrapping a handkerchief round his hand, cursing healthily. The woman in ankle boots was standing stock still, as though frozen by the passage of time. The two boys had vanished in pursuit, and the man with the Flying Scotsman was sitting amidst the wreckage scratching his head in disbelief. The hamster seemed to have disappeared completely.

In the absence of the principal character, everything began to slow down. The two boys came back disconsolately. The young assistant came to life and returned to the counter, as did I, and started to book people in and out again. An air of uncertain calm reigned. The lady with the ankle boots came to, and went out pushing a number of books down into her shopping bag. The one remaining lady still sitting on the counter came gingerly down, and sidled out as quickly as possible. Silence reigned. Those of us who were left stood waiting for a renewal of hostilities. The hamster seemed to have vanished off the face of the earth. It couldn't have beaten a retreat into a skirting board, for the library was comparatively new, and had concrete walls right down to the floor. The floor itself was parquet all over.

We all stared about watchfully. It had to be somewhere. A sudden roar heralded the end. The Flying Scotsman, still sitting on the floor, was writhing about. The hamster, following its exploits with the ankle boot lady, had clearly taken to the nether regions, and had nipped smartly up his trouser leg, like a train into a tunnel. He leapt to his feet, trod firmly on what was left of his model train, swore fluently, and shook the animal out – whereupon it was caught immediately in the boy's bag. The siege of the branch library was over. Hugh grabbed both boys and rapidly ejected them. The Flying Scotsman salvaged what was left of his model, and beat a hasty retreat, muttering. I decided it was time for tea-break. The peaceful life of the provinces was far too much for me.

14

Upstairs, Downstairs

Beaver said: "At last you won't be the new boy any more. Someone called Alec Foster is starting on Monday."

He wasn't replacing anyone. We had simply been understaffed for a long time, and now we were getting an addition.

"Is he married?" asked Jill and Janet in unison.

"No – he's nineteen, dark-haired, and plays in a pop group," replied Beaver. Tovey grinned.

"Just your sort, Janet."

Janet went slightly pink. She was still a schoolgirl. She still wore a schoolgirl's cardigan, schoolgirl's flat shoes, schoolgirl's unmade-up face. You couldn't yet imagine what Janet's sort was.

We all waited, with different reasons, for Monday. Tovey waited, because more help made life easier. Bill waited, for exactly the same reason. Beaver waited, because it gave him someone else to boss around. Chiltern waited, because he never did anything else. The girls waited, to see if he *was* their type. And I waited, for the sheer joy of finding someone junior to myself.

Monday eight-forty-five came, and Alec Foster didn't. Tovey, as usual, didn't work Monday morning, so it was Beaver who felt put out. Jill also wasn't working that Monday morning, so it was left to Janet to look depressed.

At eight-fifty-five, he came in. He certainly looked different from the rest of us. We were all dressed fairly soberly, if casually. Alec was miles ahead in fashion terms. We all felt ten years older immediately.

"Am I late? Sorry," he said cheerfully to Beaver.

Beaver, who had expected a timid apology, had the wind taken out of his sails.

"What happened?" he asked.

"I don't know. What has happened?" replied Alec innocently.

"You're late; don't let it happen again," squeaked Beaver, sounding like a walking cliché. "You sign in here; put eight-fifty-five."

"Sign in?" said Alec incredulously. "Sounds like the Civil Service."

"This is Local Government. You are a Local Government Officer," said Beaver stiffly.

"Strewth," said Alec inelegantly.

I looked at Janet, who was examining a book extremely intently. I could see why she was having to look hard; it was upside down.

After lunch Tovey appeared, had a few words with Alec, and called me over.

"Keep an eye on Alec, would you? In fact, you could first of all take these delivery notes to Mr Stuart – take Alec with you."

Mr Stewart was, I very well knew, the janitor. I hadn't visited him in his lair since the incident of the mysterious puddle, and we had always been rather wary of each other since that confrontation. It struck me as rather odd that the janitor might want the delivery notes, but with Alec next to me, expecting me to know my way about, it hardly seemed the right moment to ask such a basic question. Accordingly I took the notes from Tovey as though it were the most natural thing in the world.

"Come along Alec," I said knowledgeably.

Alec said, "Why are we going down these stairs?"

I said, "Ah."

I couldn't think of a reason, to save my life. Rapidly, I cast around in my mind. Could it be that Mr Stewart's job was to stamp all incoming mail with the time and date? It seemed reasonable. But it couldn't be true, if I thought for a moment. It was inconceivable that I could have worked there for eight months and not known that.

Or perhaps he was going to deliver them to one of the branch libraries? I had a brief but delicious vision of old Mr Stewart, a roll of pin-ups stuck to his saddle-bag, chugging around the district on a moped. But no, I couldn't believe that either. Anyway, one glance at the delivery notes told me that they were certainly for us; they covered all the books that had come in from the local bookseller the previous week. I still couldn't think of a cogent reason.

"Things," I said darkly, "are never what they seem."

I received a distinctly blank look from Alec as we descended the stairs, but the problem didn't perplex him for long, as he suddenly found himself deeply involved with the pin-ups. Matters of Local Governmental procedure were receding from his mind at a rate of knots. We reached Mr Stewart, sitting exactly as I had last seen him, reading the *Daily Mirror,* smoking, and looking like Buddha.

"Good afternoon young man. No, good afternoon young *men,*" he exclaimed with a faint welcoming smile, " . . . and what can I do for you?"

His slightly eloquent air obviously took Alec a little by surprise. Mr Stewart had not always been a caretaker; it was a retirement job, and rumour had it that he had been quite a successful businessman in his time. He was certainly ready to bandy words with anyone, and had a wry sense of humour when he felt like it.

"I've just brought these delivery notes down for you," I said, with as much confidence as I could muster.

"That's very good of you. For me, are they? What a surprise. Well I never."

I was a little discomforted by this somewhat condescending reception, but I didn't know him very well, and decided it was probably just his way.

"That was just his way," I muttered to Alec as we clambered back up the stairs.

"Yes – but why were they for him? It seems quite extraordinary." Alec was quite right; it did seem quite extraordinary.

"I've no idea what he does with them; but we always take them down there," I replied bravely, hoping that that was the end of it. Privately I determined to find out exactly what he did with them as soon as possible, even if it meant asking Jill. As we emerged, Tovey was waiting for us.

"Whatever have you been doing down there?" he asked. I sensed trouble.

"Just taking the delivery notes to Mr Stewart," I replied, sounding confident, feeling anything but.

"Mr Stewart?" Tovey laughed out loud. "Whatever would the caretaker do with a bundle of delivery notes?"

I felt rather hurt by all this. He had, after all, sent me down with them. And now he was asking the same question that had been exercising me for the last five minutes, and which I had been trying to avoid.

"You said – take them to Mr Stewart," I said, feeling both cross and sheepish at the same time, and attempting not to show either. "Not that Mr Stewart, you fool," said Tovey, still laughing, "Mr Stuart – upstairs, in cataloguing."

As soon as he repeated the name, I fell in. It was the easiest mistake in the world to make. I knew the other Mr Stuart upstairs perfectly well, of course. For some reason I shall never understand, when Tovey said Stuart, my mind had simply leapt to the wrong one. Mr Stuart was the clerk upstairs whom I had never had much to do with, but whom on retrospect was quite obviously exactly the person to deal with delivery notes. I set off downstairs (to recover the delivery notes), then upstairs (to deliver them). Alec trailed behind.

Mr Stewart (downstairs) said, "Hello again, young men, I've finished with these now, thank you very much."

Mr Stuart (upstairs) said, "I start work as the janitor next week, did you know?" (Typical of Tovey, I thought. Told the whole place by now.)

Alec said, "That's the best thing that's happened since I've been here. Can we do it again tomorrow?"

I had started off to impress. And I had. But not in quite the way I had intended. I'd been there nearly eight months, and Alec had been there half a day. So far, he was one up.

15

Arsenic and Old Books

The library was never very busy during the daytime in the week, except for a small flurry around lunch time, and the usual outbreak of chaos when the children came in after school.

Consequently we tended to know all the regulars, and even when we didn't know them, we knew what sort of people they were. Young mothers, with babies left in prams in the hall. Middle-aged chars, coming in more for a quiet gossip and a bit of warm than anything else. Elderly spinsters, looking for the inevitable love-stories. Old age pensioners, of both sexes. Students, of varying colours, hovering around the law shelves, the economics shelves, and the history shelves. The occasional shopgirl or boy, darting in during a break.

Anyone outside these categories, we always tended to notice. At least, I did. Jill never seemed to be looking beyond her own fingernails. Chiltern would sit impassive, treating the public like the sea, which continually washed up against him, but had no lasting effect. Janet was giving most of her attention to Alec, who wasn't giving a great deal of it back. Beaver in his high-pitched way strode about, huge trousers flapping, looking important, but never looking anyone in the eye in case they asked him a question. Bill Davies concentrated heavily on the stockroom and his curls of smoke.

Tovey was the only one I felt who did keep an eye on our clientèle. He treated life as something of a game, to be played with the least exertion possible, providing you still won. He watched everything with a slightly cynical eye, accepting things as they came, looking for no trouble. Consequently, when I began to suspect some-thing about one of our readers, it was to Tovey that I was preparing to go – although I knew he wouldn't be very easy to activate. But I wasn't ready yet.

The reader in question was a man of about thirty-five years old. I first noticed him one Friday afternoon, about half-past two. He didn't fit into any of our categories; that was not too unusual in itself – we often had the odd exception in, away from work through sickness, or official sickness. It was only when I saw him twice more the following week that I began to wonder. He was looking perfectly fit, so I judged him to have moved out of my mental category of people just finishing being ill.

He was dressed casually, and had an intense, slightly worried, look about him. Perhaps he was on holiday? Or perhaps he had lost his job? Speculation was idle, I decided, but I cast a closer-than-usual eye over the books he was taking out. They gave me a mild surprise. All four were non-fiction, and all four were to do with chemistry. Nothing very startling about that, except that he didn't look like a chemist, and was certainly too old to be a student.

I looked at his tickets. Charles Levett, they said, unhelpfully. The name meant nothing to me. The next time he came in, I watched a little more closely. He seemed to have lost interest in chemistry, and was now hovering around the law section. It made a change from Messrs Okimbu and Kassim, I thought. Finally, he settled for four books on common law; *Law for the Layman, How to use a Solicitor, The Processes of Law, Sentences and Appeals.*

After he had put these four down on the counter, he produced a fifth, which I hadn't noticed him selecting. It didn't seem to fit at all. It was a slim, red volume, entitled Needlework for Beginners. This really began to worry me.

What could it all add up to? What possible sort of life would a man lead that made him make such an ap-parently unconnected series of books?

My mind took off on a sudden flight of fancy; I had it. He was, or was going to be, a *criminal.*

"Don't be ridiculous," I said to myself, "You're getting over-dramatic."

"Just consider," I answered. "Four books on chemistry – in other words, poison; then four books on law – how to deal with arrest, if it comes; then one on needlework – preparing for mailbags."

I looked at myself, mentally, in derision. You ought to be locked away in the Juvenile department, I told myself sternly. You're right, I agreed, thinking I probably was. Nevertheless, I knew I was going to watch Charles Levett's next selection with close interest.

It was a month before he was back, paying his overdue fines without complaint, though I half expected a blow over the head for daring to ask for money from him. To Jill Shaw's total astonishment, I offered to help her on the 'Out' counter when Levett arrived there. It didn't take much persuasion. I watched with interest. He appeared, with just two books. Both were about South America.

That did it. He was clearly planning his getaway. I had to speak to Tovey. I was aware that he would automatically pooh-pooh the whole idea, so I made myself look intensely serious when I accosted him.

"Mr Tovey, I think – I don't know, you understand, but I think – we may have a potential felon among the readers."

"They're all bloody felons, if you ask me," said Tovey lugubriously. "Which particular character have you in mind?"

"Levett – Charles Levett."

"Never heard of him."

"Well, I think you're going to," I said darkly. "I'll point him out to you next time he comes in."

"What's he *done*?" asked Tovey, coming, reasonably, to the point.

"I don't know whether he's *done* anything; it's what he's going to do. He could be going to poison his wife." I

94

had said more than I had intended to say. Despite myself, my tongue had run away with itself. But it was too late now. Tovey gave me one of those rather pitying looks which suggested pretty clearly he had come to the conclusion that I had finally gone off my head.

"I hesitate to use this expression," he said heavily, "but have you any *evidence*?" I told him about the sequence of books.

"Good grief; if we put the fuzz onto everyone who came in here, simply through analysing their reading, we'd never stop. Half the adult population would be inside for sexual offences, another quarter would be under suspicion for reading about great criminals of the past, and the rest would be had up for loitering. Go away, and look up these bloody reservations."

I felt rather hurt by this. Perhaps my imagination had run away with me. The trouble was, once the idea had lodged itself there, it obstinately refused to go away, and every new turn of events seemed just to confirm the suspicion. I was simply behaving like a responsible citizen, I told myself, and this was all the thanks I got. I determined to collect some more evidence. Then, if need be, I'd go direct to the chief. I was not going to let a villain get away with it, just because Tovey was determined to turn a blind eye.

Typically, then, Levett vanished. That is to say, I didn't see him for about two months. Whether in fact he had been in and out regularly, but I had missed him due to the rather odd hours we worked, or whether he had simply not been coming I couldn't tell.

Apart from the odd caustic remark from Tovey – "How's the underworld then?", or "Gone to ground has he?", the subject was left in abeyance. But when he came back, he came with a vengeance. He obviously had access to a large number of tickets – through wife, children, aged in-laws – I couldn't tell what. But when he appeared, he brought a very large and mixed bag of books with him, some of which he had had a remarkably long time. To give him credit, they had all been renewed; he wasn't contravening *our* laws at all.

But when I looked at the titles: the books on common law were back; so too were the books on chemistry. The needlework book was there – but so were some others. Some books on gardening, for instance (I had read enough detective fiction to know that certain weedkillers could also be administered to humans).

A book on the human anatomy. A book on "Carving the Sunday joint". A book on Egyptology (embalming?). A book on the laws of emigration and extradition. I had to be right. No man in his right mind would have collected that lot for himself without some criminal intent. The titles alone told the story loud and clear. Somehow I had to get Tovey interested.

I took a note of all the titles, looked hard again at Charles Levett's face (that was not a sane man, not if I knew one) and decided to force the issue. I showed him the list, ready to threaten him with the chief if he wouldn't take it seriously. But he had to agree, it was a *bit* odd. He looked up Charles Levett's original application from in our index.

"Well, he's been coming about two years; can't say I've ever noticed him myself. Got no bad notes on the form." (We attached a note to the application form if they were consistently offending the rules). "Lives in a good area." (Money troubles, I wondered?) "I'll see if Bill knows anything about him." He summoned Bill Davies. No, Bill had never noticed him either. Yes, he did agree it was all rather out of the ordinary.

"I could just have a word with the nick," offered Bill, hopefully.

It struck me that Bill was exactly the person to know someone from the local nick. The niceties of librarianship, he didn't want to know about. The peripheries, such as knowing the odd policeman, or carpenter, or doctor, or butcher who came in regularly – he could be relied on for. Tovey was worried by this development.

"It starts to get official then; we could be very embarrassed if we aren't careful."

"What about talking to the chief, then?" I asked, playing my card.

Tovey and Bill looked at each other. Clearly, that was what ought to be done. But somehow, neither wanted to involve him. He'd either be totally disinterested, and stop the whole proceedings (and even Tovey was interested enough by now to want it to develop one way or another); or, more likely, he'd say leave it to him, and we'd never hear another word about it.

"It's academic," said Tovey suddenly, "The chief's away anyway." It was true; we'd all forgotten, but he had just gone off to Spain for his fortnight's holiday.

"That settles it," said Bill. "I'll talk to old Marchant. He's the station Sergeant."

"Do it unofficially, for God's sake," said Tovey frowning.

"I'll just have a drink with him and sound him out," said Bill. "In fact, I might as well go now – he's probably in the boozer already." Right in character, I thought, for Bill. Any remotely legitimate chance to skip off, and he'd skip.

"OK," said Tovey, heavily, thinking exactly what I was thinking. "And mind – take it easy." I thought that "take it easy", was the last thing you'd have to remind Bill to do, but he nodded responsibly.

"Leave it to me. I'll ask him so quietly he won't even notice he's replied." And he went off. Tovey and I looked at each other, wondering.

At that minute, Charles Levett appeared with the books he wanted to take out. And those books threw us both. In our suspicious state, they were the last thing we would have expected. Two books by Georgette Heyer; Elizabethan love stories, both. It was more puzzling by the minute.

Rather to my irritation, it didn't look as though I was going to see Bill again that day. I was finishing at lunchtime, and by lunchtime Bill hadn't come back. I lived near enough, and was interested enough, to drop in at tea-time. I found Bill and Tovey in conversation.

"Well?" I asked, scarcely able to contain myself. They looked at each other.

"Well," said Bill, "Marchant's quite interested. He wants us to let him know next time Levett's in. And in the meantime, he's going to see if he's got any form." He pronounced the word 'form' with slight embarrassment; it was the right word, but even Bill, always ready with the offbeat word (despite his appearance), felt uneasy saying it. I was too involved even to think of smiling at it.

"It might be too late by then," I said.

"There's not much else we can do," said Tovey practically.

"We can hardly send the fuzz around to his house, saying 'I understand you've been taking some funny books out of the library. Would I be right in believing you're a potential murderer?', now could we?"

I had to agree Tovey was right. There was nothing we could do but wait. We didn't have to wait very long. Not even until Levett came in again. Because before he did, the station sergeant did. He had a funny smile around his mouth.

"Anything to report?" asked Tovey.

"Well," said Marchant, "I can tell you this much. He's got no form behind him." We all looked a little disappointed.

"I can tell you a bit more. Or rather, make a suggestion. Keep an eye on the *Radio Times*." Tovey got there first. But then, so he should. He'd been in the business a lot longer than I.

"Don't tell me," he said, "I know what he is. He's a writer." And, of course, as soon as he said it, it was obvious. We kept an eye on the *Radio Times*.

Sure enough, "Written by Charles Levett" appeared quite often. He had simply been gleaning information for his hundred and one plots.

Once we got over our initial sense of foolishness, we all became rather proud of him. We even told him about it one day. But one thing puzzled us, and we asked him. "What about the sewing book? And the Georgette Heyers?" That was obvious too, once you knew it. His mum lived with them. And she liked a good read.

16

The Golden Rule

Occasionally, I would go in to the library determined that today I would win a spiritual crown. Nothing would be too much trouble. A reader would only have to hint at a need, and I would be there, ready to help. All things were possible, and it would be a very difficult request indeed which would beat me.

On such a day, Mrs Watson came in. She appeared with a large hold-all, fixed to a metal wheel trolley, and from it she produced seven books. She handed them all back, and then said, "My husband wants to read *The Jealous God . . .*"

"Ah, yes," I interrupted, "I'll see if we've got a copy in."

I walked off in the direction of the catalogue, to discover, as I had half-expected, that it was fiction – and to find the name of the author required a visit upstairs to the BNB.

"Shan't keep you a moment," I said breezily as I hurried past.

"But . . ." she started. But I had gone.

I quickly tracked it down, returned down stairs, went to its place on the shelves under 'B' (for John Braine) and found, as one always does, that it was out.

"It doesn't seem to be in," I called, "I'll just check whether it has come back today." It hadn't.

"I'll just check whether it's got in the non-fiction by mistake."

"Ah, but . . ." But I was gone.

I didn't know quite *how* to check if it had got in the non-fiction by mistake – because of course there were literally thousands of places it could be in there. However, I had a vague hunt round, checked the returned shelves, and the one place I thought a book of that title might be lurking. It wasn't.

"Sorry, I can't track it down at the moment" Mrs Watson said, "Look, you mustn't . . ." But it was one of those days, and I was determined to worry.

"It's possible it has just returned from the bookbinders; I'll just check in the stockroom."

Mrs Watson watched me go, looking, I thought, rather impressed at my determination not to be defeated. It wasn't in the stockroom among the returned rebound books; neither was it among the damaged stock. A thought struck me. I went back.

"It's not . . ." I said hesitantly, "It's not a, a, a *rude* book, is it? Not one we might keep out of reach of children, for example?"

"Certainly not, what do you take my husband for?"

"I just thought it might have been one of those we normally keep in the office. It doesn't say 'Shelve in office', does it?"

"Not as far as I know."

"Ah. Well let me just see if one of the branches has it in stock."

"I don't think you understand . . ." Mrs Watson began again.

"Yes I do, perfectly. We're not too busy at the moment – I really do have the time to hunt for it. If you don't mind waiting, that is?"

"It just seems so unnecessary," she said.

"Don't you worry," I said kindly. I rang up the largest of our branches. No, it wasn't in at the moment. I rang a second branch, No, they didn't have it either. I thought I'd better check just which branches actually possessed the book.

"Shan't keep you a moment," I said again, buzzing by, on my way upstairs. "Really . . ." But I was gone.

I discovered what I thought I might discover; that all branches officially had a copy – but as I rang each one up in turn, they were all already out on loan. I came downstairs again.

"Well, I'm sorry, I can't raise one anywhere. We only have the one copy ourselves, and I really can't tell you where that is at the moment. It must be out on loan somewhere. I'll have to reserve it for you. It shouldn't take too long."

"Reserve it?"

"Yes – if we can just fill this form in, next time the book comes in we'll send you the card, and keep it for you." I went across to the other side of the counter, took a Reserve card from the Readers' Enquiry desk, and returned with it. On the counter, in front of Mrs Watson, lay a book. I looked at it. It was called *The Jealous God*. I looked at Mrs Watson. She looked back.

"Wherever did you find it?" I asked, totally at a loss.

"In my bag."

"In your bag?" I repeated idiotically.

"Yes. I've already read it; now my husband wants to read it. I just want to take it back again."

"But I've just spent the last twenty minutes looking for it . . ."

"I kept trying to tell you, only you were being so busy you didn't seem to want to listen."

Feeling acutely silly, I booked *The Jealous God* out to Mrs Watson again, and retired to the tea-room to lick my wounds. So much, I thought, for being determined to win a 'be good to the readers' prize.

I was still not feeling too well disposed to readers a few days afterwards when I had one of my very few quarrels with the public.

There was a notice, and rule, which said 'SILENCE'. It was not something I had ever questioned, or anyone else had ever questioned. It had always seemed natural to keep fairly quiet in the library, and most people seemed to feel the same way. Which made it the more surprising when two people, a man and a woman of about thirty, came in talking loudly. To be fair, people quite often got as far as the counter noisily, but when they passed through the gate into the lending section itself, the noise subsided. But not this day. I soon realized, as they arrived at the counter, that they were in the middle of a row.

"It's absolutely no good going on like that. I haven't changed my mind, and I've no intention of doing so now, or at any other time, for that matter."

"Well, I think it's utterly unreasonable. You've never seen it my way, not for a moment. You've never even tried just to *imagine* I could be right." They arrived at the counter. I kept my eyes down, presuming they would stop without my help. They didn't.

"I don't think you've got any right to go about it that way, and if it were my dog, I'd be furious."

"Well, it isn't your dog, is it?"

"All right, it isn't. But that doesn't alter the principle."

I had taken their books by now, and handed over their tickets to them. I felt it was now time for silence. As, however, they didn't seem to be sharing that feeling, I thought I'd better take a little action. Unfortunately, I wasn't very clear what action to take. To cough a little, and indicate with my eyes the notice which said 'SILENCE' seemed a little stagey. However, as I didn't have much time to think of anything else, I tried it. I needn't have bothered.

"It would be exactly the same if it were a cat."

"Or a goat perhaps? Or an Aberdeen Angus cow, or bull, or whatever they are?"

I had coughed during the goat bit, and glanced meaningfully at the notice during the Aberdeen Angus bit. Beyond looking at me for a split second as I coughed, they totally ignored me, and passed on into the library, in full spate.

"You're just looking for trouble, bringing all those animals into it . . ." I heard, as they disappeared from view.

I looked across the counter, into the office. Tovey had

obviously heard the contretemps too, because he made a face at me and gestured after them in a way which said quite clearly "Get after them and shut them up." Feeling ill-prepared to act as a marriage counsellor, I got after them, fearing that I wasn't going to be very successful.

They had gone right past the returned books section, and had settled near the do-it-yourself department. They were beginning to collect a small but interested audience. A library, I realized with passing interest, was an ideal place to listen to someone else's conversation, because all you have to do is take a book from the shelves, stand still, and listen. So far three people were doing this, and one, with a little more sense of theatre, was standing round the other side of the book stack, taking one or two books out, and peering through the gap he was causing.

"It doesn't alter the fact that you were being basically unkind . . ."

"It doesn't alter the fact that *you* were being bloody rude . . ." it went on.

Looking at the audience, I felt something of a spoilsport butting in. I was also, I had to admit, rather enjoying it myself. I couldn't really understand the row at all; it seemed to be one of those rows about rows – like politicians having talks about talks. What I really wanted to do was to take a book off the shelves, open it, and listen too. Unfortunately, that didn't coincide with what Tovey wanted.

"Well, I shall tell him you do it, and if I know him at all, he'll explode."

"If he does explode, it'll be your fault. Don't let's have any mistake about that."

It was clearly not going to subside of its own accord; I had to speak.

"Excuse me, but would you mind being quieter please. We do have a rule of silence in here," I said tentatively, and very publicly.

I don't know what I had expected exactly, but it was

certainly not what I got. They both turned to look at me, and the man said, "Why?"

"Yes, why?" echoed the woman.

I heard a small cough/explosion behind me. The smell told me that if I turned round towards the stockroom, which was immediately behind me, I'd see a curl of smoke. The cough/explosion was Bill Davies thoroughly enjoying himself at my expense. And didn't I hear a slight titter from the other side of the book stack?

"Well, it's the rule," I said feebly. "I don't make the rules."

"If you can explain exactly why we should be quiet, we might," said the man.

"Yes," said the woman, suddenly joining forces with him, "why exactly should we be quiet?"

I really was at a loss. Why indeed should they be quiet? No-one could honestly pretend that absolute silence was essential to the choosing of books – particularly as there was always a small hubbub of chatter from the charladies – of whom there were always some present. Even so, I had to follow the party line.

"There always has been a silence rule in here, as in all public libraries – so that people can have quiet while they are choosing their books."

"Yes, but why?"

"Why?"

I sensed I was on dangerous ground, and looked for the coward's way out.

"Look, as I said, I don't make the rules. There *is* a rule which says silence. If you aren't prepared to follow the rules, you must either leave the library, or take the matter up with the librarian in charge."

I felt rather pleased with what, to me, seemed a rather articulate piece of brinksmanship. I was hopeful that the sheer number of words might deflect them from their purpose; which seemed to be to have a quarrel with someone – if not with themselves, then with someone else. Namely, me.

"Pathetic," said the man.

"Yes, pathetic," echoed his better, or worse, half.

"Mind you, it's just what you'd expect from a petty local-government mind."

I thought that was really hitting below the belt. I had had no desire at all to be a Local Government Officer. In fact, until I received my terms of employment from the borough, I didn't even know I was. All I had wanted to do was work in a library; and here I was, a local government official on the one hand (even belonging to the union NALGO), and a law enforcer (unsuccessful) on the other.

"It really isn't fair to everyone else; or indeed me," I said, feeling the whole thing was getting out of hand. The charade was getting me nowhere. I knew it, they knew it, and they knew I knew it. But I had reached the point of no return; I had to risk everything.

"I shall have to ask you to leave; will you please go now."

I had by now gathered a few more spectators. They had given up all pretence at looking at books, and were just standing watching the floor show. As I said it, I had absolutely no idea what was going to happen as a result. I had been led, willy-nilly, into a position where that was all I had left to say. And now that I had said it, I had no intimation at all of the reaction I was going to get – except that I didn't feel too confident.

What did happen next was a surprise to us all. It took the form of a long wail, followed by a catastrophic tumbling sound from the other side of the library as we heard about four hundred books land on the floor, closely followed by a child of about four. Its mother had come to watch the fun, and the child itself had gone mountaineering up the nearest book stack, which for some unaccountable reason hadn't been properly fixed, and had promptly collapsed.

We all rushed round to sort out the wreckage, including my quarrelsome twosome. They were as helpful as everyone else, helping the rescue of the bawling infant, pulling the books off it, and dragging the offending book stack to one side. The mother was helping matters by comforting the child until it stopped wailing, then telling it off so that it started again.

I imagined that in the face of disaster, the whole unsatisfactory episode which had gone before might be forgotten and the problem removed. In a sense, it was. They stopped quarrelling with each other. And they stopped arguing with me about the merits and demerits of the need for quietness in the library. Instead, the man turned to me again and said "Now perhaps you can just explain exactly why this extremely unsafe bookcase is allowed in this library?" I felt I had had about enough.

"Frankly, I can't. It's hardly intentional, as you might imagine for yourself."

"Well, I'm not satisfied. I want to see someone in charge." I introduced them to Tovey.

"These people want to know why the book stack collapsed. They were also the ones who were making all the noise and pointblank refusing to stop. You could say they caused the whole thing," I added maliciously, "because they were the cause of the mother leaving the child in the first place."

"Ah," said Tovey, "how interesting. We have a few rights, this side of the counter, you know. One of which is to refuse to allow members of the public whom we do not consider responsible to take books out of the library. I think I consider you are in that category. Would you hand me your tickets, please?" Tovey, I thought, could be quite impressive, when he put his mind to it. So, evidently, did they.

"You fool," said the man to the woman.

"It's your fault; I told you you shouldn't have touched that dog," said the woman.

"It would have been all the same if it had been the cat . . . " said the man.

"Thank you," said Tovey sweetly, taking the tickets.

"Blooming good riddance," I said, slightly too loudly. Tovey looked at me.

"Just observe the 'Silence' rule, will you?" he said.

17

The Biter Bit

Bill Davies was an entertainment in himself. He was entirely different from Jill Shaw, yet they had one thing in common. They didn't like work. The difference was that whereas Jill made no bones about it, and resolutely ignored it as much as she could, Bill was a much smoother operator.

Jill carried the art of not noticing someone who was leaning over the counter, desperately trying to attract her attention, to a remarkable degree. She could be blind, deaf and dumb when the occasion required it of her. Which, being her, it often did.

Bill, on the other hand, had a much more complex problem. He didn't want to do anything, but he didn't want to show it. He was also in the remarkable position of having most of the borough believing he was the chief librarian – a belief he wanted to do nothing to discourage. So his act was to look helpful, and impressive, but always to find a reason why he, at the particular moment, couldn't actually help himself. He would, however, most certainly find someone who could help. He had perfected this act years before I had joined, but it took me some months to realize how well he practised it.

Occasionally, though, his artistry caught up with him. He was standing one day in the centre of the counter area, ostensibly 'checking'. What he was actually doing was nothing; just standing there.

I was working at the incoming counter, Chiltern at the outgoing, and Janet was seated at the Readers' Enquiry desk. Bill stood still, looking as though he were trying to decide which of several immensely important matters he had to attend to first.

In came an old lady, who could scarcely believe her luck when she spied Bill. He normally kept out of her way, because he knew that all she really wanted to do was talk to him, under the guise of asking his advice about what to read next, or what not to read next. However, just as she spied him, he also spied her, and moved like lightning towards the switchboard. It was easy to pick up the phone, press a lever or two, and make it seem as though he were in earnest conversation with someone of considerable importance. Bill was a past master at this.

However, this time it went wrong right from the outset; for no sooner had he reached the switchboard and picked up the phone than it started to buzz.

This was not part of his plan at all; he could hardly ignore it, though – and anyway, if he had, he would have been forced to deal with the old lady instead. "Central Library," he said, rather discouragingly, into the mouthpiece. I couldn't hear the reply, but by his face I suspected it was something like "Here is Mr Okimbu".

"Oh yes," parried Bill, "I'll just put you on to the assistant responsible for that . . . "

But before he could get away, the voice pressed on. Bill's face grew crosser. He put his hand over the mouthpiece, and muttered to me, "Wants to speak to the Chief Librarian."

I stifled a grin to myself. Bill was clearly now in two minds.

On one hand he thoroughly enjoyed being thought of as the chief; but on the other he didn't want to be landed with any trouble. Plus the additional fact that no-one was supposed to be put through to the chief if it could be humanly avoided. All lending library problems should be sorted out by the lending library, said the system. Bill looked round, like a cornered rat. The old lady was still waiting, so he decided to take a chance. "Can I help?" he asked authoritatively into the phone.

He was thus pursuing his usual policy of not admitting he was the boss, but not giving anything away either. Bill listened for a few moments, and I realized he was regretting his choice. He started shuffling around, looking, I suspected, for Beaver. Beaver, though, was not to be seen, and Bill was stuck.

"Ah, I see," he said. "I'm not sure I shall be able to help you there myself, because I wasn't the person responsible for sending out that particular letter." I began to realize what it was all about. Letters, in the tone that Bill was using, meant almost invariably one thing: after an overdue card had gone out to remind readers to bring books back, the next step, if that had had no effect, was a letter. A vaguely threatening letter, suggesting that if they didn't take some action soon, and bring the books back, the council would have no option but to commence legal proceedings against them.

We never liked sending these letters out, because if we were in the wrong (and inevitably sometimes we were), people became very irritated, and no-one liked dealing with these confrontations. The particularly funny thing in this case was that Bill had sent the letter himself. But he wasn't going to admit to that.

The person on the telephone obviously wasn't going to be shuffled off quite so easily, and Bill had to listen a little longer before he managed to lay the receiver down, and look around for someone to pass the whole tiresome business on to. I suddenly became extraordinarily busy; Chiltern suddenly became extraordinarily busy; and Janet suddenly became extraordinarily busy. All at the same time. Wasn't that remarkable? Bill started to leave the counter, whereupon he was pounced on by the old lady who had been lurking behind a pillar.

"Ah, Mr Davies, so glad you have got a moment, I wonder whether . . . "

"I'm sorry, Mrs Freeth, I'm on the telephone at the moment," said Bill. Mrs Freeth looked disbelievingly at him, perfectly able to see that he wasn't on the telephone at that moment at all. Bill gestured towards the switch-

110

board. "Just sorting something out," he explained, and hurried away. He didn't hurry very far, though, because at that precise moment the chief appeared at the bottom of the stairs, and accosted him.

"Ah, Beaver, I wonder if you've got a minute?"

"No, actually, Mr Mortimore, I'm just on the phone to a reader . . ."

"Good," said Mr Mortimore, "would you just come upstairs with me please." Bill was now well and truly caught.

He couldn't in all conscience leave the reader on the end of the phone. If he wavered at all, Mrs Freeth would grab him. And it was impossible to explain any of it to the chief at all. But it did give him one let out, he realized. "Mr Hornsby," he called, "I've just got to go upstairs with Mr Mortimore. Could you help the gentleman on the phone?" I cursed silently. Bill had done it again. And he hadn't even given me any information, which meant I had to begin all over again with an already irate customer. I thought I had better make it seem as though we weren't all totally incompetent, so I said, "Can you let me have the *exact* details, please?" As I had suspected, it was a threatening letter – that by the sound of it should not have been sent at all. But I wasn't going to be outplayed by Bill quite that easily.

"It will take a little time to check it all out," I said. "If you could give me your number, we can ring back when we have sorted out the position."

I was rather pleased by that. It meant that I had for once not been landed in trouble by someone else, and that I could put Bill back onto it when he returned. Unfortunately I was counting my chickens before they were hatched.

"Oh no, I've been caught with that one before. All that will happen is that you'll put the phone down and I shall never hear another thing. Please put me back to the man I started to deal with. I take it he is the chief librarian?" I didn't see how I could dodge this one.

"Well, actually, he isn't."

"Well, then, who is?"

"Mr Mortimore."

"In that case please let me speak to him."

"Well, Mr Mortimore doesn't usually deal with this sort of matter."

"Look here, young man, I have a letter signed by Mr Mortimore threatening to take legal action against me if I don't bring these books back – which incidentally I *did* bring back two months ago. If Mr Mortimore is going to write to me like that, I demand the right to speak to him." I tended to agree. It seemed pointless, anyway, to try to explain that Mr Mortimore's name appeared in print at the bottom of every letter that left the library, whether he had anything to do with it or not. It was just the usual bureaucratic way of doing things. I didn't seem to have much option.

"If you hold on I'll try and connect you," I said, persuading my hand to press the button we were never supposed to press.

The chief snapped out an irritated "Yes?"

"Er, Mr Mortimore, it's Hornsby . . . " I started.

"I don't normally speak to members of the public," he said, in a much gentler tone, "if you just wait a moment I'll get a member of my staff to come to the phone and help you."

"No, Mr Mortimore, I work in the library. I've just got a very irate reader who wants to talk to you about a summons letter we sent out."

"But you know I never talk to people about those things."

"Yes, but they are insisting; they say it's got your name on the bottom, and they want to talk to you about it."

"Whose job is it?"

"Mr Davies's."

"Well, find him and put him on to it."

"But you've got Mr Davies with you now . . . "

"Have I? Good Lord. I'll send him down to see to it," and he put the phone down. "He's just coming now," I said into the phone, carefully not revealing who 'he' was. Bill came down the stairs, looking wary, to be intercepted by Mrs Freeth again.

"I'm sorry, Mrs Freeth, but I'm still on the phone."

"Are you trying to avoid me, Mr Davies?"

"No, of course not – I'll come out as soon as I've finished." Bill entered the counter area, picked up the phone, and continued negotiations. Soon he had to leave the counter to check on the letters file in the office. On his way, he smiled at Mrs Freeth, still waiting; indicated he was still on the phone; turned round, and stepped straight on Susan, Mrs Bell's dog. Not realizing for a moment which dog it was, or for that matter that it was a dog at all, Bill got as far as saying, "Stupid bitch ... " when he froze in horror as he recognized the fur coat accompanying the lady accompanying the dog.

"Mr Davies," barked Mrs Bell, appropriately, "you've trodden on Susan!"

"Oh Lord," muttered Bill, "I seem to be putting my foot in it everywhere this morning."

"I beg your pardon?" said Mrs Bell, failing to appreciate the unintentional joke. "Well, seeing as you're here, I've just got this little list. Perhaps you could help me find Lytton Strachey's memoirs?"

Bill looked at Mrs Bell, grand and imperious before him. He looked at Mrs Freeth, still lurking in the wings by the pillar. He looked down at Susan, who was looking up hungrily. He looked towards the switchboard, which was waiting threateningly. They seemed to be closing in on him from all sides. In a moment of panic, he decided to make a run for it. He set off with considerable speed towards the door of the stockroom, clearly with the aim of putting the word 'PRIVATE' between him and all the forces of the world which were besieging him. Unfortunately, as he reached the last book stack before the stockroom, a small child chose that precise moment to back out suddenly in his path, and Bill administered a firm, and completely unplanned, kick in its rear. The child instantly burst into a howl of anguish, and the mother hurtled along towards it, castigating Bill at the same time as enquiring just how much the nasty man had really hurt him.

At the sound of the din, Tovey came out of the stockroom, closely followed by Jill, who for once in her life did something useful and diverted the mother's attention by picking the bawling child up.

Bill decided the best thing he could do was to get back to the switchboard, where, among all the pandemonium all around him, he felt most safe. Taking the easy way out, and with absolutely no checking at all, he said to the irate telephoner, "I'm extremely sorry, you are absolutely right. I do hope you can understand it is possible to make the occasional organizational error." The other end of the telephone seemed mollified, because I heard Bill apologizing again, and saying "Goodbye" extremely quietly. When he had finished talking, he flipped the levers up again, but continued to use the receiver as though it were still live. Clearly, his instinct for self-preservation hadn't left him yet.

Unfortunately, the chief hadn't left him either, because he chose that exact moment to come into the counter. He took one look at Bill and the switchboard, and said loudly, "Davies, I should have thought you'd have known by now. If neither lever is up or down, you are not connected. You are talking to yourself." Bill looked thoroughly crestfallen at this piece of out-manoeuvring.

"And if you *have* finished," went on Mr Mortimore, "perhaps you'd come back upstairs with me."

Thus, probably for the only time in his life, Bill had been saved by authority taking a hand and giving him more work to do. As he trailed upstairs behind the chief I could almost see him saying prayers of thanks. Janet, Chiltern and I had thoroughly enjoyed the whole episode; we felt that for once the biter had been bit. Regrettably we weren't left to enjoy it for long, because Mrs Freeth bore down on Janet and Mrs Bell bore down on me. You always have to pay in the end.

18

New Words for Old

One day, a new word entered our vocabulary. It was to alter our lives. I overheard Tovey talking to Beaver:

"He's talking about photocharging," I heard him mutter. I didn't know who 'he' was, and I didn't know what photocharging was, but it seemed worth repeating.

"Tovey says he's talking about photocharging," I reported to Janet.

"What's that?" she asked immediately, not giving me a clue, or a moment to prepare an answer. I had to admit I didn't know.

"Well, *who's* talking about it then?" she asked. I had to admit I didn't know that either.

"That's not really a very revealing piece of information then, is it?" said Janet, who was by now certainly not the shy schoolgirl she had been when I joined.

"There's no need to be quite so sharp," I said, feeling more annoyed with myself than her. "It could be very important."

"Well, seeing as you don't know what it's about, and you don't know who said it, we can't really tell, can we?" She gave her grin, which made it seem less sharp than it had sounded. She had, after all, a point. I spied Beaver wandering about, and thought I'd try the direct question.

"Do you know what photocharging is?" I asked innocently.

"Yes, thanks," he said, flapping off at speed.

I was beginning to feel rather annoyed. For one reason or another, I wasn't getting anywhere. And more than that, people were scoring off me into the bargain. I could

115

hardly go up to Tovey and say "I was listening to what you were telling Beaver, and I couldn't quite understand it. Please explain it." I looked it up in the dictionary. It wasn't there. I asked Jill. She'd never heard of it. I asked Bill. "Oh, *you've* heard, have you?" was all I could get out of him. Beyond the certain knowledge that something was in the air, I was getting no wiser at all. Curiously, it was Colin of Cataloguing who finally told me, one tea-time.

"Well, how are you looking forward to photo-charging?" he asked me, friendly for once. I thought I'd better be honest.

"I don't really know what it is," I replied.

"Oh, you must get Tovey to tell you about it."

"He's not on this afternoon – can't you give me some idea?"

"You're going to give up the Browne system down-stairs, and go over to photocharging instead."

I knew that the Browne system was the method we used of tucking the book tickets into the readers' tickets, so we knew who had which book out. But I still hadn't much idea what photocharging was.

"Whatever is it?"

Colin was just going, so he said briefly, "Basically, you store the information on what book it is, and which reader is taking it out, on microfilm, instead of all that ticket-tucking and filing you have to do. There's a big camera thing going to be installed downstairs on the out counter – that does it all."

"You mean – no more searching for tickets in the trays when books come back? No more ticket filing?"

"That's right."

"I can't believe it."

"Well, it's going to happen. Should be in in about six weeks."

Colin went, leaving me astonished. The palaver of filing every ticket for every book that went out of the library each night seemed as inescapable a part of running the library as shelving the books themselves.

And those frantic searches for tickets that never seemed to be in their places – that too seemed part of the very bone-structure of the library. And, more important still, I knew about photocharging – and most of the other juniors didn't.

"Well, thank goodness I won't be doing this much longer," I said to Chiltern next day as I was searching for a lost ticket. Chiltern stared at me suspiciously.

"What do you mean?"

"I've had enough of this ridiculous searching for tickets that are never there, and that absurd filing system we have to use every night, getting all the tickets in all those trays."

"Are you leaving, or what?"

"I reckon I can stand just about another six weeks of it, and that's going to be that."

Chiltern continued to stare at me suspiciously, but then the phone buzzed, and I was able to go away and answer it without divulging my secret. As I talked on the phone, I could see Chiltern talking to Janet, and looking furtively in my direction.

"What's it all about?" asked Janet when I had finished.

"It's the book issue filing system; I've decided I've had enough of it. It's an archaic idea; all those silly tickets in those silly trays." My rather childish game didn't last very long, however, because Tovey had heard part of my conversation, and came up full of the news.

"You've heard then?" he asked.

"Heard what?" said Janet and Chiltern in unison.

"Wasn't he telling you? No more filing. No more ticket searching. No more issuing as we know it."

"I don't understand," said Janet, looking bewildered.

"Uh?" muttered Chiltern eloquently.

"We're going over to photocharging," said Tovey proudly, "that'll change all our lives somewhat." Now they both looked silently puzzled.

"Mind you, there'll be some rather boring preliminaries; we'll have to write the number of every book in the library in the top right hand corner of the flyleaf of each one . . . "

"Every book?" asked Janet incredulously.

"Every one. And we'll have to make out new tickets – no, *a* new ticket – for every reader we have. But it'll all be worth it in the end."

Janet still hadn't got over the first preliminary. "Let me get this right," she said. "Each book in the library will have to have the numbers of all the other books written in it?"

"No, you young idiot," said Tovey condescendingly. "Each book just has its own number on the flyleaf."

"I still don't understand," wailed Janet. "Can you *explain?* What *is* photocharging?"

"It's quite simple. We have a large camera fixed over there," Tovey pointed to the end of the 'Out' counter. "When someone takes a book out, they just give you the book and their ticket, and you press a button and photograph the number of the book, with the ticket next to it. So all the details are on microfilm."

"No date-stamping then? So how do they know when the books are due back?"

"Ah," said Tovey, a little less happily. "We put a small ticket in the pocket of the book when it goes out, with the date stamped on that."

"On the pocket?" asked Chiltern, looking dazed.

"No, on the card, you chump," said Tovey.

"So there *is* date-stamping?" said Chiltern, recovering himself rapidly.

"Yes – but the real advantage is when the books come back. All we have to do is look at the date ticket, to see it's not overdue – and the customers can go in. They keep their ticket with them all the time, so you can discharge the books in seconds."

Chiltern's mind was, for once, at work.

"But if they keep their tickets all the time, there's no limit to the number of books they can take out?"

"Er, true," said Tovey, momentarily disconcerted.

"And that means Mr Okimbu can take the entire law

118

library home with him," I went on cheerfully.

"Er, yes, that's true too," said Tovey, even more disconcerted.

"How will it work then?" asked Janet.

"Well . . ." said Tovey, extemporizing like mad, "we won't let them take out more than the normal number at any one time. And trust them after that . . ." he finished weakly.

"How many of our loyal readers do you trust?" I asked innocently.

"Not a bloody one," said Tovey, recovering his usual tone.

"But we'll just have to live with it. I don't expect too many will take advantage." I wasn't too sure of that. Neither was Chiltern, nor Janet. But we realized, as Tovey had said, we'd just have to live with it and trust them. At least the books would be read, rather than standing dustily about on the shelves. But there were, as Tovey had said, some boring preliminaries. Not least of which was transcribing the number of every book by hand onto the top right-hand corner of the flyleaves. I rediscovered how incredibly dirty books were – particularly of course those which seldom moved from their shelves. I never knew how many books there were in our particular library, but there were thousands upon thousands.

One of the jobs we had to do, in addition to writing the number on, was at the same time to remove the now redundant date leaf that was stuck in every book. It was interesting in doing so to see when each book last went out. Some hadn't moved literally for years, whilst others must have been in and out every few days. One particular book I had an interest in was a learned book my brother had written a number of years earlier. I was pleased to find that although like many of the more erudite books we carried it was hardly worn out from over-use, it had nevertheless had a steady readership over the years.

No exercise at the library could go on for very long

without some diversion, and the numbering of books was no exception. Tovey had explained to me that in addition to the numbering, we had to remove each date leaf. He had not, however, explained this to Chiltern – who, on finding book after book without a date page in them, decided to use his initiative and put one in. So for a whole afternoon I ripped page after page out, while Chiltern stuck page after page in – and then Tovey, on checking, would rip them out again.

"Remarkable how many books have never been out at all," he observed, staring at one date-stamp-free page after another. It was only when he came across two copies of *The Cruel Sea*, which despite being the most popular book in the library, had apparently never been out, that he realized something was wrong. Chiltern went a deeper shade of red than usual when it was explained to him.

But the real excitement started when the photo-charging machine itself arrived. It was surprisingly large and heavy; but it had, after all, to accommodate not only the camera and lens, but also a hefty base plate to rest the book (and itself) on, plus a small battery of lights to illuminate the pages as well.

It was installed, to the accompaniment of much carpentry, into the 'Out' counter, and sat there brooding for about a week before it was finally assembled and wired up. No-one was ready for it when it happened. It was a quiet Thursday afternoon when it was finally ready for use. We had a small collection of regulars in at the time; a few chars, one or two early schoolchildren, a couple of young mothers, with babies asleep in their prams in the lobby, an old-age pensioner, and a nun. All was peaceful. I was looking for some reservations, and Jill was lethargically doing some shelving, when suddenly the air was rent with a thunderclap. Both babies started crying instantly, the old-age pensioner sat down hurriedly on a windowsill, Jill dropped her books, the chars dropped automatically to their knees, and the nun crossed herself.

"What in Heaven's name – oh sorry Sister – whatever

was that?" said Bill, emerging from the stockroom so fast he brought three curls of smoke with him.

"Perhaps Tovey's shot himself," said Jill, recovering nastily.

We converged on the counter, to find an electrician and a rather dazed-looking Tovey, together with Beaver, all wearing that rather sheepish look of pleasure some people put on when hearing bad news.

"What's happened?" we all asked at once.

Tovey tried to look nonchalant. "Just giving the photocharger a dry run," said he airily. Although his rather white face belied the airiness.

"Was that it?" asked Bill incredulously.

"That was it," said Tovey shakily. "Let me demonstrate." He placed a book on the baseplate, laid a ticket next to it, and pressed a button. The thunderclap struck again, together with a blinding flash of light. It was all over in a split second; but it was, to say the least, dramatic.

"Gordon Bennet," said Bill, mixing his ancestries, "are we going to have to live with that?"

"I'm afraid you are," said Tovey. "You'll get used to it."

"It's a case of having to, I suppose," said Bill gloomily. "Can I have a go?"

"Help yourself." Bill pressed the button, recoiling as the thunder crashed and the lightning struck. By now we had the entire collection of the public watching.

"I call it disgraceful," said one of the chars.

"They don't think of us old 'uns," said the other.

"Reminds me of the war," said the old-age pensioner.

"Eeeeouuuuugh," said one of the babies.

"Urgle," the other agreed.

"Gordon Bennet," said Bill again, "I think I'd rather have the tickets."

19

Lightning Changes

Once the photocharging machine was installed, the next step was to introduce the idea to the public.

"It'll be a bloody disaster," Tovey said gloomily. "Worse than bloody reservations."

"Talking of which," I asked, "how do we do them – if there aren't any tickets to check through?" Tovey stared at me in an uncomprehending way.

"How do we do reservations?" he repeated blankly. "I've no idea. How do we do reservations, Beaver?" Beaver, to Tovey's annoyance, knew. He had been to library school rather more recently than Tovey, and photocharging had been invented by then.

"It's very simple; you make a list of every book that's reserved, then you check every book that comes in against the list."

"That's all, is it?" Tovey looked, and sounded, sarcastic. "You look at every bloody book to see if it is reserved?"

"Yes."

"It's worse than the last bloody system."

"I don't think so . . ." Beaver began knowledgeably.

"Well, I *do*," said Tovey firmly.

"No," said Beaver, not sensing when to keep quiet, "it's a very easy matter once you get used to it. It just takes a bit of time, that's all."

"I should think it does take a bit of bloody time – and don't you go telling me it'll be all right when I get used to it." Tovey looked extremely vexed. Mostly, I thought, because he hadn't thought of the problem before.

122

We issued a leaflet explaining the new system in as simple a way as possible. To see some of the older people staring at it, turning it first one way and then another, then screwing up their eyes disbelievingly, made me wonder how they ever got through the books they took home.

The first step we had to take which affected the readers was to issue each of them with a new ticket, clearly written on a white background so that it would photograph easily. We started issuing the new tickets a week before the new system came into operation – telling them not to use it yet, but always to bring it with them in future. Needless to say, for months after, we had people arriving with the old tickets, who were then extremely cross because we couldn't do anything to help them.

As we were *photographing* the tickets, naturally each reader needed only one – which we photographed in turn against every book he or she took out. One extremely cantankerous old gentleman totally refused to understand the idea.

"You've only given me one ticket," he said.

"You're only going to need one ticket."

"But I take four books out."

"Yes, but you'll only need one ticket."

"Four books, four tickets."

"No – one ticket. We photograph the one ticket against each book."

"How can I take out four books if I've only got one ticket?"

"I've just said – we photograph the same ticket each time."

"Photograph? I'm taking books out, not photographs."

"I know you're taking books out. We photograph the number of the book, together with your ticket."

"I've told you the number of books – four – that's why I want four tickets."

"No, you don't need four tickets. Look – I put your

ticket next to the book number here, and photograph it. Then I put your same ticket next to the number of the next book, and photograph *that*. Now do you see?"

"What do you want to go photographing it for?"

"We keep a record of who has what book on film."

"I'm not taking any books out on films."

"It doesn't matter what books you are taking – we just keep a record."

"I'm not taking records either."

"No, of course you're not."

"Is this a record library then?"

"No."

"But if you keep records – you just said you keep records – can't I take them out? I've got a diamond stylus."

"No. Please look again." I went through the whole rigmarole once more. It seemed childishly easy to me.

"Oh, I see." Thank goodness, I thought gratefully.

"I see – and then you use my ordinary tickets just like you used to as well," he finished triumphantly. I had to give up.

"You just use your tickets normally for today – then when the new system starts next week, bring your new white ticket in, and we'll demonstrate exactly what happens." He seemed to understand that, at least, and stumped off shaking his head.

"What's this?" enquired Chiltern, seconds after he had gone, and knowing exactly what it was.

"It's his ticket," I replied wearily. "After all that, he's managed to leave it behind. We'll have to keep it for him – though I expect he'll think he's lost it and never come in again." I spoke too soon; he reappeared almost immediately.

"I thought you said I had to bring my new ticket in next week," he said crossly. "How can I if you're keeping it here?" It was amazing how, innocent as we were, it seemed to be our fault entirely.

It was the first day of the new system. I woke up

knowing it was going to be terrible. And I wasn't far wrong. To start with, the continual thunder and lightning of the machine itself took a great deal of getting used to. As we got more dexterous with placing book, ticket, and date card all in a line to be photographed together, the machine gun fire rattled out with ever increasing rapidity. Quite simply, the library never sounded the same again. If my earlier expectations of the library being a peaceful place to work in had been even remotely right before, they were certainly misplaced now.

But getting used to the noise was one thing; getting everyone through the system was quite another. Although we had already issued hundreds of the new tickets, nearly everyone who came in seemed only to have the old ones still. As no-one could be issued with books until they possessed a new white ticket to be photographed, we had to make them out while they waited – and not surprisingly a long queue soon formed at the going out counter.

"What's all this for then?" they would ask.

"To speed things up," we would reply.

"But we've been ten minutes in this queue," they would reply.

"It won't happen after this first time," we would reply, rashly. Which was utterly untrue, because for weeks and weeks people seemed to be trickling – or on Saturdays, surging – in with old tickets. And the same queue kept forming.

"Still speeding things up?" people would ask sarcastically.

"It'll be all right in the end."

"If we all last till then."

20

A Pint of Pigs over the Frog and Toad

Bill Davies called me out of the office into the counter.

"Could you take over here for a few minutes?" That was a familiar enough request, particularly from Bill. What came next, though, wasn't familiar at all.

"I'm just going over the frog," he added. I looked at him dubiously. Had he finally flipped? Had the persistent dodging of work and shuffling off of problems finally blown his mind for good and all?

"I'm sorry?" I said, more politely than I felt.

"Going over the frog." I couldn't think of any suitable reply. I looked at Tovey for help. He obviously hadn't noticed anything.

"That's OK, Ken," he said, "go and stand in for Bill for five minutes."

I decided this usage of the word 'frog' must have been one of those small pieces of knowledge that I had somehow missed at school. (I had, believe it or not, missed learning how to write, too. "I was away when they learned joined-up," I used to say, proudly, whenever someone was rude about my handwriting – which was often. Someone had thoughtlessly tripped me up outside the school gates, and I was away for three months with a bad fracture. During which time everyone had learned to write.)

I went on the counter, joining Chiltern and Alec. In a lull, I said to Chiltern, "Do you know where Bill's gone?"

"Out, I think" said Chiltern, unhelpfully.

"Aha, that's all you know," I said mysteriously. Then to Alec, "Do *you* know where he's gone?"

"No idea," said Alec, more conversationally, but still not very interested.

"Allow me to tell you," I said pompously.

"Mmm?" they both said, in a bored sort of tone.

"Over the frog," I announced grandly. Chiltern looked at me blankly.

"Over the *frog*? It doesn't mean anything."

"Yes it does," said Alec in an unnecessarily scornful way. "It means over the road. I expect he's gone to the tobacconist."

"Over the *road*?" exclaimed Chiltern and I simultaneously. "What are you talking about?"

"Explain yourself."

Alec took a deep breath, as if explaining something painfully simple to an unresponsive child. "It's rhyming slang – frog and toad – road. Really it's over the frog and toad, only they shorten it to frog."

And that was how it all began. One of the more mystifying phases that the public of that borough went through as they visited us, for a long time. The whole idea of 'over the frog' grabbed my imagination instantly, and I quickly spread it around. It was soon the latest rage. It spread like wild-fire. We asked Bill for some more examples. We picked up some more from other people. And Chiltern even discovered a rhyming-slang dictionary in the library itself (something it hadn't occurred to me even to look for. But then, I only worked there). We began to prepare the most complicated sentences and try them out on each other, but soon it inevitably spread to dealing with the public.

"I'm sorry, I'll have to hand you over to Mr Davies here, I'm just off for my Jim Skinner," I said to an outraged Mrs Bell, one day.

"He means his dinner," said Bill soothingly to her, shaking his head, as though he couldn't imagine what young people were coming to today. I popped back.

"I might be a little late back, I'm afraid, Mr Davies – I'm having my Barnet done." That was a particularly unfair one. Because Barnet was an adjoining borough to

ours, and Mrs Bell clearly thought – not surprisingly –
that I was saying something about that. It was left to Bill
to say to her "He means he's having his hair cut. Barnet
Fair – hair." Mrs Bell looked even more indignant than
she usually did, and proceeded to take Bill on a long and
fruitless tour of the library looking for a book that had
been missing for three years.

The reason that Tovey hadn't seemed particularly
surprised at Bill's original remark was, I discovered later,
because he was quite a rhyming-slang artist in his own
right. Whenever he wanted to, he was perfectly able to
surround himself with an impenetrable blanket of slang,
which you had to work very hard at indeed to make any
sense of at all.

"Coming for a tumble?" he'd call out, to the con-
sternation of any spinsters who may be within earshot.

"Yes, I wouldn't mind a pint of pigs," I'd reply
happily. ('Tumble' was short for 'tumble down the sink'
– or drink. 'Pint of pigs' meant pint of beer – 'pigs'
being short for 'pig's ear'.)

"We're just going down the field of wheat – coming?"
we'd call to Chiltern – which didn't refer to a pub of
that name, but really meant 'down the street'.

Janet looked upon the whole thing with a certain air
of detached amusement, but at the same time gave the
firm impression that she considered it all a trifle childish.
Jill decided the whole thing was beneath her. But as, in
order to join in, she would have to expend a certain
amount of energy and learn something, it was not surprising she took no great interest. Chiltern, on the other
hand, took a great deal of interest. Always capable of
surprise, he had been the one to sort out the dictionary,
and he worked hard and long at it. It was exactly the
kind of thing which would tickle his somewhat quirky
mind, and he took great delight in throwing us all into
total confusion.

"I'm going off to an itch and scratch tonight," he'd
say airily (meaning match).

Or, answering the phone, and calling out to whomever was on the incoming side of the counter, "Mrs Devereaux has lost her Joe Rook" (book). Or "Anyone fancy some horse and carts tonight?" (darts). Occasionally we could find a reply, but the whole subject came to a grinding halt the day Chiltern arrived with something he'd clearly spent most of the previous night working on.

He burst in a minute or so late, and said for all to hear, "Ooh – I had a jack the ripper before the jeremiah, a quick jennie lea, then a laugh and joke. Picked up some needle and thread from the longacre, and I'm sorry if I'm 'Arry Tate." I looked at Alec, stupefied. I then looked past Alec, even more stupefied, because behind him the chief stood, drinking it all in. Or to put it another way, standing agasp.

"Whatever are you talking about Beaver?" he enquired, getting the name wrong as usual. Chiltern went an unhealthy shade of red.

"Um, it's rhyming slang, Sir," he said, hoping that was going to be enough. It wasn't.

"I'm perfectly well aware what it is," said the chief (which I was prepared to bet a pound he wasn't), "but I wish to know what it means."

Chiltern took this to mean that all was not lost, and that Mr Mortimore was actually mildly interested.

"Well, Sir . . ." he began.

"Yes, yes," said Mr Mortimore impatiently.

"It meant I had a kipper in front of the fire, a quick cup of tea and a smoke; I bought some bread from the baker, and I'm sorry if I'm late."

"Yes, yes, well I suspect you're a Holy Friar, but we won't dwell on that," said the chief astonishingly. He looked round at us all. "A gypsies warning to you all," he said amiably, and wandered off, a trace of a smile on his face.

I looked at Chiltern enquiringly. We all looked at Chiltern; he had become our expert translator. He looked shocked.

"He thinks I'm a liar – and wishes us good morning."

"He's nobody's two-foot rule," I said proudly.

But it was the end somehow. After all, knowing he knew what he knew, you'd never have the West Ham reserve, would you?

21

The Deep Waters of Initiative

Tovey said, "Well, you've done one branch, in a manner of speaking. How about trying another? They've got sickness at Lansdowne Road." So I went to the Lansdowne Road branch, about four miles away.

My last visit to a branch I remembered well; so did all the readers who had been there at the time. It is not, after all, every day that the entire collection of library inhabitants can be terrorized by one small hamster, or that the results of months of careful model-building can be reduced to matchwood in an instant. I hoped for nothing like so dramatic a day.

I arrived to find they really had sickness. It was a smaller branch even than the previous one I had gone to; the normal staff on duty never amounted to more than three – and at this moment in time was down to one. She was called Joanna, and was a woman of about forty. Pleasant, helpful, and efficient. It should be, I thought, an enjoyable day, with just enough difference and informality about it to provide something of a holiday atmosphere. I would have nothing to do other than straightforward counter work, and with a branch that size, the two of us should cope easily enough. As we did, all morning.

I soon found my way around adequately. As before, I took a certain amount of pleasure in being able to walk into a totally unknown place, and within minutes know more about where to find a certain book than most of the readers who might have been coming there regularly for years.

At twelve o'clock, Joanna suggested I went to lunch.

"I can manage for an hour," she said, "and Philip Jeffreys will be arriving at one – and the two of you can handle the afternoon. I'll come back at five, and you can go off then."

"Are you sure you can manage alone for now?" I asked.

"Yes – it's quiet in here before lunch. But you'll need the two of you at one o'clock."

So I got in my old car, and chugged off. I chugged back again just before one, to find Joanna sitting peacefully by the telephone, with perhaps half a dozen readers scattered throughout the library.

"Philip?" I enquired (I had never met him before).

"Not arrived yet," she said. "I expect he'll be here in a moment." She pottered off into the staff-room, leaving me alone. It was an experience I'd never had before. I looked around my territory. It seemed quiet enough, and just for a moment, I was master of all I surveyed. One o'clock came, and Joanna returned, ready to go.

"No Philip yet?" she asked.

"Apparently not."

"Perhaps I'd better hang on till he arrives."

"Is he reliable?" I asked.

"Oh yes."

"Well, you go then. I'll be OK for a few minutes." She looked a bit reluctant.

"Go on," I said, "you've got to be back by five anyway; have *some* afternoon free. I can manage for a few moments." She looked round the library.

"Well, it doesn't seem very busy. All right. I expect he'll be along any minute." And she went.

I had another look at all I surveyed. It occurred to me that I had no idea what Philip looked like, or how old he was. I wondered what sort of afternoon I was going to have. While I was wondering, the phone rang.

"Oh," it said, surprised, "that's not Miss Wakefield, is it?"

"No," I said truthfully, "it isn't. Can I help you?"

"Who is it then?"

"My name's Hornsby."

"Who are you?"

"I've just said; my name's Hornsby."

"Yes, I heard that – but *who* are you?" Realizing at last what he meant, I explained I was here for the day only.

"But if you want one of the regular assistants, I'm expecting Mr Jeffreys any minute – can I get him to ring you back?"

"Hardly – I *am* Mr Jeffreys. I just rang to say I think I've got this bug too. I hoped to catch Joanna before she went. I'm sorry about the short notice. I'd expected to be OK, but when I put my coat on to come out, I realized I wasn't OK at all. Sorry about that." I was rather sorry about that too.

"You'd better see if you can get some help from the Central Library," Philip went on, "you won't be able to manage by yourself."

"Right," I said, the idea forming in my head that I was going to have a jolly good try. "Well, I hope you feel better soon."

"So do I," he said gloomily, "you feel so ill feeling ill." We said our goodbyes, and put our phones down.

I looked round what was now without any question my territory, and decided this was the moment to make my name. The time when one person ran a branch single-handed for one whole afternoon. It was all still looking reasonably peaceful. The public fell into their recognizable pattern; a char, two middle-aged women, one with a child, an old-age pensioner, and a student of about eighteen rummaging among the books on English Literature.

A few more people came in, a few went out. Most of them looked at me with a little curiosity, not knowing me. But no-one said anything, or asked anything diffi-cult. It was now a quarter past one, and Joanna's threatened one-o'clock rush didn't seem to be happening.

The phone rang. It seemed a pretty standard sort of question; had we a certain book on crochet? I didn't know off-hand, I said, but I'd go and look. I went off towards the catalogue, noticing as I did that simultaneously someone wanted to come in and someone wanted to go out. Wasn't that just like life, I thought?

"Won't be a second," I said to them both, and hurried to the catalogue. Yes, apparently we did possess the book. I went to its appointed place on the shelves, and – of course – it wasn't in. I thought I could just let the people in and out, and then return to the telephone. But it wasn't as easy as that. The incoming lady said "We've just got an *au pair* over from France, and I'd like her to be able to take some books out while she's here. Can you tell me what the formalities are?" I knew the answer, but it wasn't a very quick one. "Ah – can you just wait a moment then. Let me just deal with that lady."

I went to the other side of the counter to let the woman out; an operation which should have taken all of five seconds. "I vould vish to orter some pooks" said the should-have-been-five-seconds lady. I was beginning to feel slightly hemmed in. However, I felt it was all small and intimate enough for me to explain out loud.

"I seem to be doing three things at once," I started apologetically, "could you both just hang on while I finish on the telephone, then I'll deal with you in turn."

"Right," said the first lady accommodatingly.

"Sorry?" said the second lady, clearly not understanding. "I vish to orter some pooks."

"Yes," I said, "I'll be with you in a second." I went back to the telephone.

"Hullo, I'm sorry to have kept you . . ." I realized I was speaking to a dead phone. She had obviously had enough of waiting. Thinking it was a trifle embarrassing, although not exactly inconvenient, I put the phone down, and returned to my first lady, who by now had a small queue behind her.

"Perhaps it might be a good idea if you went through and chose your own books for the moment, and I'll come and find you when it's a little quieter."

"I don't really want any books myself," she said,

rather inconsiderately, I thought.

"Ah." An idea struck me. "In that case, let your *au pair* take her books out on your tickets now, and you can get some tickets for her next time you come in."

"No, my son wants my tickets for his student books."

"I am shtill vaiting," floated the words from the other side.

"Just coming," I said, wishing it were true. I then had another brainwave.

"If you like to come in the counter," I said to the *au pair* lady, "perhaps you could fill the form in yourself while I sort these other people out?" She seemed quite happy at that, and came in and settled down at our desk inside the counter. Breathing a sigh of relief, I let the queue in (fortunately none of them raised any problems) and went to the foreign lady.

"Now, what did you want to reserve?"

"I vish to orter Florence Greenberg's Jewish Cookery pook." I knew that book. I also knew Florence Greenberg had written more than one of them.

"Yes, but which one?"

"Florence Greenberg's. I chust sait."

"Yes, but she has written more than one. Do you know which one it is you want?" Falling into the common trap, I had by now begun to raise my voice – as one often does when talking to a foreigner who doesn't appear to be understanding.

"Do not chout at me, yunk man. I am not teaf." I was receiving a little attention from the other occupants of the library by now.

"Sorry, I'm just trying to find out which Florence Greenberg book you mean."

"Sorry?" I decided the only thing to do was to demonstrate.

"Will you come with me?" I led her to the catalogue, to the accompaniment of the phone, which had chosen that precise moment to buzz. I thought I'd ignore it. I looked up Greenberg, and found there was only one listed. Of course, I thought to myself. Typical, I muttered.

"Sorry?" she enquired.

I tried to explain that where I came from – the main central library – we had several different Florence Greenberg cookery books. I hadn't realized they had only the one at this particular branch library. It seemed impossible to explain that I did in fact know what I was talking about. Quite simply, she had decided I was out of my mind. I also couldn't ignore the phone any longer. I left the foreign lady looking dazed and puzzled, and returned to the buzzing machine. It was my crochet lady.

"I'm sorry I was so long," I said, and explained we were rather short-staffed. I also explained that the book was out at the moment.

"It's very urgent," she said, "do you think any of your other libraries would have it in?"

I couldn't for the life of me understand how a book on crochet could be very urgent, but I didn't feel it was up to me to question it. And her request was perfectly reasonable.

"If you hold on, I'll ring the central library on the other line, and see if they have it." I dialled my own library. Jill Shaw answered it.

"Ken Hornsby . . ." I began.

"Not here," said Jill.

"I know . . ." I began again.

"He's at the Lansdowne Road branch," she said, and put the phone down. I rang again.

"This *is* Ken Hornsby speaking," I said firmly, feeling like Henry Hall. "I want to know if you have a particular book on crochet in at the moment." Jill went off to look, and I laid the phone down on the counter. I was about to return to my Florence Greenberg lady, still looking mildly stupefied, when I realized there was someone waiting to go out.

"Do you just want to go out?" I asked. It seemed rather a silly question to anyone who wouldn't know the point behind it, or what chaos could be caused if there was yet another odd question lurking.

"Yes." A second person joined the 'Out' queue. I decided drastic situations demanded drastic measures.

"If you'd just like to stamp the books yourselves – there's the date stamp – and tuck the card into the ticket and leave it on the counter – you'll get out rather quicker than if you wait for me," I said, putting on a vaguely conspiratorial smile, which I hoped also said "We're all in this together".

The two in the queue looked extremely surprised, but appeared to grasp the situation. They both went inside the counter (which I hadn't expected, and didn't seem strictly necessary) and started stamping.

I went back to my foreigner, and disappeared with her round the shelves, to check that Florence Greenberg wasn't in her place on the shelf all the time.

I had by now forgotten about Jill, but she for once hadn't forgotten about me. After saying my name and getting no response, she started whistling down the phone and clicking it. This made a surprising amount of noise, and I looked across to the counter, just in time to see an obliging member of the public who had recently arrived at the 'In' counter picking up the phone and talking into it. He had had to lean across rather a long way, and in order to facilitate his conversation with Jill walked round the counter to get nearer to the switch-board. By now the two would-be leavers had finished stamping their own books, but had discovered what I had forgotten – namely that they couldn't get out of the library until I pressed the exit gate release button. So one of them was back inside the counter looking for the button, while, just to help everything along, the other was stamping someone else's book for them.

At that moment, Tovey walked in. He looked around him in amazement. He looked at one member of the public, on our telephone in our counter. He looked at another member of the public, sitting at our desk, making out forms. He looked at another member of the public, searching on hands and knees for the floor button which would let him out. He looked at another member of the public stamping out books for yet another member of the public. And he looked, unsuccessfully, for me.

The first intimation I had of his arrival was a well-known voice saying "What the bl——, what the hell's going on?" I returned to the counter, leaving Florence Greenberg stranded again.

"Been busy," I said weakly.

"So it would appear," said Tovey, rather unnecessarily sarcastically, I thought.

"I am vishing to orter a pook," said a voice plaintively at my side, recognizing that authority had arrived.

"We can't get out," said a queue.

"It's for you," said a voice, holding out the telephone.

"I think I've done it now," said the scribe at the desk, "is it all right?"

Slowly we sorted out the little dramas. When it was all over, Tovey looked at me.

"There's something about you. You come over here. To the most peaceful branch in the whole system. And within minutes you've turned it into a complete maelstrom. How do you do it?"

I thought this was very unfair, and said so. I was, after all, only showing a little initiative in getting the public to help themselves, rather than wait impatiently in a queue like a lot of irate sheep.

"Anyway, what are you doing here?" I asked truculently, turning defence into attack.

"I've come to get a book out," said Tovey, unexpectedly. I had forgotten; it was his afternoon off. And I had also forgotten; he lived in the same road.

"I see," I said. Then, feeling a trifle embarrassed, "I suppose you're going now . . . ?" Tovey looked at me, and grinned.

"I don't feel, somehow, that would be very responsible of me. What do you think?" I thought he was probably quite right. Under the circumstances. So he waited. And I waited. And nothing else really happened.

22

Driving Instructions

One of our occupational hazards was the man, or woman, with a list in his hand. It always meant trouble; if only because it took so long to deal with. Books were never in their place, and people never understood why. Consequently we were never overwhelmed with delight at the vision of the outstretched hand and the limp piece of paper. I got thoroughly caught one morning. A man of about forty-five, wearing overalls, pottered in.

The fact that he was wearing overalls told me nothing. People, I had discovered, appeared in many clothes, and it was a total mistake to judge by appearances. The man in overalls could easily be a doctor building a bedside cabinet for his son's daughter's nursery, and just popping across the road to the library for a book on french polishing. (He wasn't, but he might have been.)

So in wandered Mr Overalls, said, "Can you help me find this?", and handed me the bit of paper. It said: "I Drive".

Assuming he wasn't simply feeling it his duty to let the local library know he has passed his driving test, and without knowing whether it was a novel or a book about road transport, or even golf, I asked "Do you know anything about it before I look it up in the catalogue?"

"Not a thing," said Mr Overalls, "they just told me you could help me find it."

I speculated for a moment on who 'they' were, decided it wouldn't materially affect the situation, and set off with him towards the catalogue. We didn't know the author, but I thought it was more likely to be about cars than an eighteenth-century love affair, and decided to short-circuit the BNB and hope to find it via the subject index. But no; it didn't appear under the driving instruction section, nor under great days of racing, nor outdoor sports (golf section).

"I'm sorry – I'll have to try upstairs. I won't keep you a moment." But it wasn't upstairs either. It wasn't a novel, and it wasn't non-fiction. In fact there was no record of a book called 'I Drive' ever having been published – either inside or outside our library. It was *The CJ's* all over again. I had to confess failure; which was rather strange. It wasn't often we could find no trace at all of a book.

"I'm sorry," I said, "but it doesn't seem to be there anywhere. Are you sure about the name?"

"Absolutely certain," he said. "Took the order myself yesterday. One yard of sand and two bags of cement – number one the Drive." It just shows how wrong it is to make assumptions. Every man who comes in clutching a piece of paper doesn't necessarily want a book.

It was Bill Davies who really started it.

The public were on the outside of the counter, and we were on the inside; a distance of about three feet apart. On a busy Saturday (all Saturdays, that meant) before photocharging set in, there were usually two of us, or even more, taking books in from the incoming readers. As the returned reader presented his or her returned books to us, we had to hunt through the trays that sat on the counter between us and them, looking for their tickets.

We had our heads down, and Bill used to talk about them; the public, that is, not the heads. He would be looking quite relaxed, occasionally passing the odd sentence in my direction. "Turned out wet again," it might look as though he were saying, as he glanced conversationally in my direction as we stood next to each other. "Silly old bat – looks as though she's just come from Dracula's castle," was usually near the truth.

"Yes, she does look about a hundred and eight," I

would reply, looking unusually grave. And then, drawing his attention to a ticket in my hand, I might add, "She must have had her face lifted seventeen times." It was most childish, and most reprehensible. To be honest, we didn't indulge in it very often, but it suddenly became a fad of the moment, and we all played it.

"What an appalling wig," said Alec to me one day as we examined a ticket together.

"Mutton dressed as lamb," I replied, turning the ticket over and looking intently at the other side.

"I wonder if he's actually got any hair at all?"

"Probably all slipped down his back."

"Could be an escaped convict."

"Or an escaped monk." I opened another book, and stared with professional interest at the blank flyleaf.

"Bet you a pound you won't ask him," I said.

"Are you an escaped monk?" said Alec very quietly indeed.

"No, I'm just bald," said the man.

"No, he's just . . ." started Alec, and then stared in horror. I stared in horror too; comprehending horror. Because I realized I was staring at a hearing aid, and a man who could lip-read. We stopped the game after that.

23

Initiation Rites

Despite the episodes at the two branch libraries I had stood in at, and despite the fact that I was nowhere near qualified and not particularly experienced, I was being thought of as a useful person in a different way from Janet, Jill, Chiltern or Alec. It was fairly simple to understand; I was older by some five years than the others. The public in general were more ready to accept me as having the right to a little authority. This was hardly fair to Janet or Jill or Chiltern, all of whom knew more about the running of a library than I did, and had had more experience.

However, the result was that when one of the ladies who ran the reference library went off for her two weeks' holiday, Tovey, in consultation with the chief, decided it was time I had a go up there. I didn't feel very well prepared for this; to start with both the real incumbents of that job were highly qualified, which seemed to me rather a basic requirement. There was nothing routine about working in the reference library. No books came or went; the job was to be ready to help with a hundred and one questions from a hundred and one people. To boot, one worked alone; the two ladies overlapped in their hours by only a few a day, so no help was at hand most of the time.

There was also a small disciplinary side to the operation, in that the desk was actually a small enclosed area at the entrance to the reference library, and no-one could enter or leave without the librarian on duty releasing the gate to let them through. (This was, of course, to prevent people quietly leaving with some

142

expensive book tucked under their coat while no-one was looking. It was also to keep undesirables out – which included unaccompanied children and tramps.)

"Do you think I can manage it?" I asked Tovey.

"We all have to go through it some time."

"Yes, but you're qualified."

"There's nothing like doing the job to learn it."

"But how can I do it if I can't do it?" It sounded rather Irish, but I knew what I meant. Tovey, on the other hand, didn't. Or didn't want to.

"Stop prevaricating. It'll be good for you." So on the following Monday I duly climbed the stairs and took my place, rather sheepishly, within the desk and mounted guard over the gate release.

I actually knew the reference library fairly well – from the customers' point of view. Whilst in the sixth form at school, and in the vacations from university, I – like many others in the same position – had used the desks there to work at. It was warm, peaceful, and every possible reference book was to hand. I had often shared my desk with various Latin textbooks, or English commentaries, and stared rather wistfully at the librarian in charge, feeling they had arrived at what must be one of the nicest jobs in the world. They had no examinations pressing ahead, no career to find and succeed in, and none of the fear of the commercial world to come looming over the horizon at some time in the future. Above all, they seemed secure, calm, and sure of what they were doing.

Now I was in that seat; and felt neither secure, nor calm, nor at all sure what I was doing. Nevertheless, I did my best to look as though it was the most natural thing in the world for me to be sitting there, and waiting for something to happen. After an hour I began to relax. Nothing much had happened. Half a dozen people had come in; none had asked me anything. One or two had wandered around the shelves (which were all around the outside, the desks and chairs being in the middle), examined a few books, presumably found what they wanted, and departed. All I had done was press the gate release some dozen times. I was even getting a little bored.

Then the post arrived. It consisted of just one large envelope, addressed to the Reference Librarian. I decided to leave it for Miss White, who would be arriving at one o'clock. I sat there for another half hour, let two more people in, decided the suspense was too much, and opened the envelope. It contained amendments to what seemed to be a Government Order. I hadn't the faintest idea what to do about it, so I left it again. It looked frightfully complicated, and had all the signs of being extremely boring. I suspected one had to run the original to earth, and then make all the amendments by hand. If that were indeed the case, I felt I would be well advised to leave it to Miss White.

"Don't just stare at it," said Mr Mortimore, just as I was staring at it. "Update it, update it." And he went as suddenly as he came. Clearly I could no longer leave it. I hadn't the remotest idea what to do next. I looked backwards behind my desk, into the cataloguing department. Seeing Colin, I subdued my pride and asked where I would find Government Orders.

"Under Government Orders. In the catalogue," he replied, nastily. "Look it up under G," he added, unnecessarily. I looked it up, found it, and ran it to earth on the shelves.

When I returned to my seat and opened it, I wasn't very pleased with what I saw. It had clearly been amended umpteen times before, and the many pages were a mish-mash of crossings out, writings in, tearings out, and stickings in. Amending it again was going to be a work of art, in more ways than one. I looked round the room. All was quiet. Rather unnervingly so. One girl student looked up at me. Aware of being on view, I lowered my head to my task. My task, though, didn't really seem to come up to the level of what one might expect the reference librarian to be doing. I got out my paste and my scissors, and started cutting up and sticking down, with the uncomfortable feeling that I looked a little ridiculous.

I looked up again. The girl student was just lowering her head, with a slight smile on her face. Feeling slightly nettled and mentally red-faced, I continued. Then the phone rang. My heart, as my mother-in-law would say, leapt off its hook. (It struck me at the time what an apt metaphor that was.)

A vaguely foreign voice asked "I want to visit some stately homes around London this coming Easter; I wonder if you could give me some addresses?" Panic immediately set in.

Where on earth do you find out details like that? Books on holidays? On walking tours? On travel? On history? On London Transport? On museums? The list could be endless, and none of them seemed particularly likely to help. I suddenly remembered a bit of odd advice Tovey had given me. "It's amazing how often the phone books can get you out of trouble." It was worth a try, I thought. How many stately homes could I actually think of? Syon House, Ham House, Hampton Court; that seemed a reasonable start. I looked them up in the phone directories, and proudly spoke the answers to the enquirer.

"Yes, I know about those," said the voice, "they're all in the phone book. I wonder what else there is?" I was wondering too. I was also feeling that that was some-thing of a blow below the belt.

"If you could hold on a moment, I'll see what else I can find," I said, sounding rather more hopeful than I felt.

I laid the phone down and thought hard. The first thing I thought was that a bit of professional help might not come amiss. I swallowed my pride and looked through into Cataloguing. Colin was nowhere to be seen. I thought I'd try Tovey. I picked up Colin's phone, and asked Janet, who answered from downstairs, if I could speak to Tovey.

"Sorry, he's already on the phone," she answered

unhelpfully, and put the phone down before I could say anything else. It was obviously up to me to think of something. I suddenly had a brainwave. Was it my imagination, or had I seen a bookrack standing alone on a windowsill, with various guides on it? I had indeed; I could even see it from where I stood. I walked over to it, with a slight lift of the spirits, aware that I might be about to solve my problem. I was just beginning to enjoy the sense of having all these books at my command. *Guides to London and Around* it said unequivocally. It even had a little index all its own, attached by a piece of string. I looked down it. "Stately Homes" leapt straight out at me, fourth on the list.

"I've made it," I thought delightedly to myself. My first success. Quite a neat little operation, I felt. The feeling didn't last long, though, because, as so often, the actual book wasn't there. There was, however, a thoughtful note tucked in where the book ought to have been. "Stately Homes", it said, "on loan to lending library". Thinking things weren't quite as bad as they might have been, I returned to the phone.

"I'm having a slight difficulty tracking the information down – but I think I've got it now. If you could just excuse me for another couple of minutes, I'll be straight back with it." The voice seemed quite happy about this, so with a glance around the room to make sure no-one was likely to want to go out for a few moments, I hurried downstairs.

"Do you know where the *Stately Homes* book is?" I panted out to Beaver, who was on the counter.

"No idea," he squeaked disinterestedly.

"Do you know?" I asked Janet.

"Try the office." That seemed a reasonable suggestion. I went in, to see Tovey still on the phone. As he didn't seem to be speaking, I mouthed at him "Are you speaking?" He shook his head. Really it was quite obvious he wasn't speaking. You could tell from the fact that he wasn't making any sound.

"Are you listening?" He nodded. That was quite

obvious too, it struck me. I hovered about for a bit. Then I began to feel this couldn't go on. I thought I'd try to communicate through his conversation. I mouthed again. "Have you seen the *Stately Homes* book?"

"What?"

"Have you seen the *Stately Homes* book?"

"What *Stately Homes* book?" he mouthed back.

"The one from upstairs."

"The one from upstairs?"

"Yes."

"Yes. You mean this one?"

He held out the book, which had been next to the telephone on his desk all the time. I nodded. It struck me in passing how surprising it was that the precise book I was after should be so near, but I was so glad to see it I didn't stop to think overmuch about it.

"Thank you," I mouthed.

"Not at all," he mouthed back. I rushed back upstairs.

"I've got it now," I said into the phone, somewhat out of breath.

"Yes?"

"Now then . . ." I started, opening the book, with the warm feeling of success inside me. I stopped. I looked at the title page again. I had missed something. It said, sure enough, "Stately Homes". What it also said, and what I had missed, was a much smaller phrase – "A guide for French visitors, in French". I opened it again. Every word was in French. I stared at it blankly.

"Hello?" said the voice.

"Um" I said, wildly.

"Are you there?"

"Yes, I'm here – it's just that, just that . . ." I tailed off, feeling utterly defeated.

"It's all in French," said the voice.

"Yes," I replied automatically.

Then I stopped. How extraordinary. How should he know that? But wait a minute, didn't I know that voice, now I thought about it? Undoubtedly I did. It was

Tovey, characteristically taking the opportunity of pulling a leg.

I felt utterly confounded and foolish. What a rotten trick, to take advantage like that. Comprehension of the whole situation came over me. The note in the book rack. The remark about the telephone directories. Tovey on the phone, not speaking. Janet putting the phone down before I could ask a question. Beaver playing disinterested. For once I recovered myself quickly. I determined not to let him realize I'd rumbled him.

"You're quite right," I said ingenuously, "it is all in French. But if you can just hang on another moment, I've another idea."

"Certainly."

I laid the phone down. For some minutes I got on with my cutting and sticking. I let two students out, and one in. I walked downstairs, and peered round the corner of the office. Tovey was still on the phone, looking slightly bored. He should have given that job to Bill, I thought. I walked back up again, and decided it was time to end it. I picked up the phone.

"Are you still on the line?" I asked.

"Yes."

"Well, I suggest you get off; there's a train coming."

I put the phone down immediately, and sat feeling extremely, childishly, pleased with myself, waiting for Tovey to roar up. Soon the phone rang. I smiled to myself.

"Reference Library," I said sweetly.

"I do not understand," said the same voice. "What is this about a train?" I was immediately in a quandary. Was Tovey carrying the joke on? Or, hot horror grabbing me, was it all genuine?

"Um," I said again, wildly.

"Sorry?"

I thought, furiously. My instinct told me it was Tovey; the evidence – though only circumstantial – told me it was Tovey. I decided to risk it.

"Don't you think we've had enough?" I asked,

sounding as self-assured as I could.

"Sorry?" that last 'Sorry' told me. I knew Tovey's voice by now when he was sending someone up.

"Mr Tovey," I said, with a mock warning note in my voice, "I think we've both had enough of this. Do you mind if I get on with some work?"

The voice gulped. I smiled to myself. It had been a war of nerves, but – just for once with Tovey – I had won.

"I should get on with some of those bloody reservations if I were you," I went on cheerily, aware that Colin had come in behind me, and feeling remarkably pleased with myself. I was feeling, and sounding, I knew, much more at home up there than I had any right to be, yet.

"You all right?" said Tovey, a yard behind me. I jumped several feet. It had not been Colin who had come in, it had been Tovey. And it had not been Tovey on the phone. The hot horror grabbed me again. I was absolutely speechless.

"What's the matter?" asked Tovey, realizing something was unquestionably wrong.

I pointed to the phone. "Can you help him?" I asked weakly. "He wants to know about stately homes." Tovey grinned, picked up a book called *Stately Homes* (in English) which had lain about eighteen inches from the phone throughout the whole episode, and spoke into the phone.

"It's OK, Colin," he said, "I think he's been initiated by now. Bye."

24

Battle of Smells

The initiation ceremony took a little getting over. I was fairly surprised at Tovey taking such an active part in it himself, and even more surprised that Colin should join in too. He had never seemed to have much in common with the rest of the staff, and the thought of him actually conniving with Tovey came as something of a shock.

It was nearly lunchtime when the charade of the stately homes was over, and by the time I had tidied away the few books that people had left on their desks, and cleared up the remnants from my cutting and sticking, Miss White had arrived for the afternoon shift. I came back in the afternoon from two to five, and spent most of the time continuing with the Government Order. The next day I was doing the opposite shift; one o'clock to eight-fifteen. The afternoon was again spent with the Government Order, tucked away in cataloguing while Miss White was on the desk, so it wasn't until five o'clock when she went home that I took my seat in the reference library again. The phone rang immediately.

"Can you tell me if there is a Mrs Hettie Cohen living at twenty-four Kenneth Grove?" it asked.

This seemed relatively easy; I looked up the local voters' lists and found that, indeed, Mrs Hettie Cohen did live at twenty-four Kenneth Grove. I wondered in passing why he wanted to know, but before I could develop my thoughts, a familiar smell manifested itself. Grape-nuts was at the gate. I could think of no reasonable reason for not letting him in, so I did so.

"So good of you, my dear boy." He settled down with a book near to an elderly lady who was studying an

150

encyclopaedia of dog care. It was difficult to tell who was the more pungent. Grape-nuts was all grape-nuts and months of neglected soap and the woman was an interesting mixture of Pekingese hair and dog food. The woman gave way first. She raised her head, looked about like a snake wondering where to strike, and quickly identified the source of the offence. She pushed her hat down more firmly over her brow, and bore down on me like the stately ship of Tarsus. She leaned over, and boomed quietly.

"Young man, would you be good enough to remove the cause of that obnoxious aroma?" She nodded her head towards Grape-nuts. I wasn't very clear what to do.

"Why?" I stalled.

"The smell is appalling."

I reflected that her dog smell hadn't come direct from a beauty soap commercial, but didn't feel able to make much capital out of that. I also didn't feel I should be taking sides.

"Well, I don't know that that is a reason for asking someone to leave."

"Of course it is; it's extremely unpleasant."

"However unpleasant it may be, there really isn't very much I can do about it."

She looked indignantly at me, then said, "If you won't, then I shall." She marched over to Grape-nuts again; at which moment the phone went once more.

"Can you tell me if a Mr Kendler lives at sixty-seven St Paul's Avenue?"

Remembering the previous enquiry, I again wondered fleetingly what it was all about. But with one eye on Grape-nuts and the ship of Tarsus, I looked up the voters' list again. As I put the phone down, I realized that events concerned with the smell were taking a more dramatic turn.

"My good lady," came the unmistakable tones of Grape-nuts, "*What* are you saying to me?"

"What I am saying is that I find it extremely disagreeable to sit next to you." By this time the entire room was alive with interest.

"What you have not said, Madam, is *why* precisely." Grape-nuts was strong enough on psychology to suspect that she wouldn't have the nerve to come right out with it. In which belief he was entirely wrong.

"Because, my man, you *smell*."

"It is extremely unlikely that I should ever be your man. And even should it, in some entirely unanticipated way, become true, I should defend my right to manage my ablutional ways precisely how I want to."

The ship of Tarsus was, to say the least, unsettled by this stream of articularity from such an entirely unexpected source. It didn't, however, halt her for long.

"You smell," she repeated, "most unpleasant, and I should be glad if you would remove yourself."

I felt a vestige of sympathy for Grape-nuts when he replied "So, Madam, do you."

This really did halt her in her tracks. Clearly, whatever outcome she had expected from her attack, she hadn't expected to have the tables turned upon her quite so thoroughly.

"I . . . *I* smell . . . ?" was all she could manage.

"If I am not much mistaken, Madam, you share your small and unimportant life with at least two dogs, and in all probability, four or six. Which is not a state of affairs you appear to be making any attempt whatever to keep to yourself, judging from the overwhelming evidence of dog and bitch on your coat, and their concomitant odour."

As I stared fascinated at the duel, the phone rang again. "Could you tell me if a Mrs or Miss Dobson lives at eighteen All Soul's Avenue?"

I was by now beginning to suspect something of a repeat performance of my initiation ceremony. However, as there seemed little I could do about it, I looked up All Soul's Avenue, and found that neither Mrs nor Miss, nor indeed Mr Dobson lived there.

"No," I said, "I'm afraid they don't."

"I wonder in that case whether you would be good

enough to have a look in the street directory and see if she is listed there. She might not have registered to vote."

Feeling that I would much rather be watching the Grape-nuts *v.* Tarsus match, I hunted out the street directory. A few sounds drifted back to me as I sat at the telephone.

"Insulting . . ."

"You were the first to commence hostilities . . ."

"Quite unprovoked . . ."

"It's a disgrace . . ."

"*I* was not unprovoked . . ."

"It's a disgrace . . ."

"There, Madam, I entirely agree . . ."

"I shall ask to have you evicted . . ."

"Nothing in the byelaws will uphold your point of view . . ."

". . . any decent citizen . . ."

". . . do you include yourself in that category?"

"Well, really . . ."

"*Really!*"

I found there was no Dobson, of any sex, at number 18 All Soul's Avenue, and said so. Grateful, the unknown inquisitor rang off.

I returned to the fray, having decided it was high time I took a hand. I walked up to them, not sure I was going to succeed, but aware that if I didn't stop it, civil war might break out.

"I'm sorry, but I shall have to ask you to leave," I said firmly. Both looked at me in astonishment.

"*Me?*" they both asked.

"Both of you. There is a silence rule here, and I am afraid in the interests of everyone else here I must ask you both to go."

I stood there, knowing it was simply a matter of wills, and that there was every chance I would lose. But what else could I do? They looked at each other. They looked at me.

"Quite disgraceful," the woman gasped.

Grape-nuts ceremoniously picked up his old paper bag and newspaper, and without a word walked quietly out. I looked at the woman expectantly. To my undying relief she did the same. I walked back to my desk.

"Fantastic," said Tovey, who had been enjoying the spectacle entirely unknown to me. The phone rang, and Tovey answered it, letting me get my breath back.

"No, I certainly won't," he said snappily. "You know perfectly well we never give that sort of answer over the phone. If you want to refer to the voters' list you have to come in and do it yourself personally." He slammed the phone down.

"I don't know why they try it on," he said to me. "Bloody hire-purchase company, checking up on whether people live at the addresses they give on their HP forms. They know we never tell them – but they keep trying it on. Some people never learn."

25

Good Deeds

"Do you know where Mrs Bell lives?" asked Beaver. I thought for a moment. Mrs Bell, of the Library Committee and the dog Susan. Yes.

"It's in Queen's Crescent, isn't it?"

"Number seventeen. She wants some books." Having said it, Beaver did a smart about-turn, and vanished in the direction of the tea-room. What did it mean? I had to ask. The only person I could see was Chiltern, so I questioned him.

"Ah, yes," he replied impassively, "she does that sometimes."

"Does what?"

"Rings up for some books. So that you take them round to her instead of her having to come out to the library. Is it raining?" I looked out of the window. It was.

"It would be," said Chiltern. "Taking advantage. I don't go along with it at all."

"I still don't understand."

Chiltern explained. She sometimes used her rank as a member of the Library Committee to get someone to take books round to her. It was a simple abuse of power, and Chiltern didn't like it. Neither did I, come to that, particularly as it looked as though I was going to be the one to go.

"Do we have to go?" I asked, feeling distinctly subversive. Chiltern explained that he had had two rows with Tovey over it, and had lost both times.

"But why don't *you* have a go? The more of us who say it, the more it will sink in." Tovey was not in that morning, so I chased after Beaver.

"This taking books round to Mrs Bell," I started, "it doesn't seem right to me. She's abusing her position, isn't she?"

"Yes," said Beaver sourly.

"Is it right that we should do it?"

"No," said Beaver, firmly getting on with something else (stirring his tea, although he didn't take sugar). He was doing all he could to discourage further discussion. For some reason, I felt truculent that morning.

"Well, I'm not going," I announced. Beaver didn't even look up.

"OK" he said, "just explain that to the chief, would you? He asked me to find someone." My truculence began to ebb. But Beaver had become interested, now that the pressure was off him.

"If you really disagree, why don't you say so? It's a free country." I looked at Chiltern.

"I don't think I'd go that far," he said, looking slightly sheepish.

I looked at them both. Chiltern was clearly ready to be impressed. Beaver didn't believe for a moment that I would take it any further, and because he wasn't instantly being obeyed, was hoping I'd give in and look feeble.

"OK," said a voice (mine, to my surprise), "I'll go and argue."

Taking a final look at both their faces, because I felt I might not see them again, I climbed the stairs and knocked on the chief's door. Nothing happened. I knocked again. Still nothing happened. Then a voice behind me said "Not in."

"Right," I said, turning round – to find it was the chief himself.

"I don't expect I can help you," he said, "I suggest you try the Lending Librarian downstairs – Mr Tovey is his name. They all know him. Tall, dark man, with glasses."

I sighed inwardly. Dealing with the chief was always the same. I had a suspicion he was worse with me than most people, though I couldn't for the life of me see why.

"No, I want to see you Mr Mortimore," I said, feeling that if I sounded his name he might get some indication that I was not a member of the public. I thought, simultaneously, that it might be to my advantage in the long run if he didn't remember who it was exactly who was refusing to go to Mrs Bell's house.

"Right-oh, Hornsby, come in."

Typical, I thought. Typical that he should choose this particular moment to get it right for once.

"What can I do for you? Is it about the County Lists?" I remembered, obscurely, that he had asked me about the County Lists the very first time we had met, in this office. It seemed to be a preoccupation of his.

"No, it's about Mrs Bell."

"Ah, yes, unusual lady. She likes Westerns, you know. Good of you to go."

I explained I was not proposing to go. That I considered it an abuse of her position to expect one of us to go. That she was in fact setting a bad example when she should have been doing the opposite. That it would be taking a member of staff away from his proper duty – when he would be needed in his rightful place behind the counter. In short, that I didn't approve and wouldn't be going. Mr Mortimore gazed at me.

"How long have you been here, laddie?" I told him, about eighteen months.

"And are you proposing to stay?" So far as I knew, I said, yes.

"We all have to do things we don't really want to, you know. Even I. I have my masters."

I said that I fully understood that, and that I had never refused to carry out a request in the past, or an order – and that I never expected to. But this was a matter of principle. Surely he must agree – it wasn't within our terms of reference to provide a personal book porterage service for members of the Library Committee who preferred not to get wet? Mr Mortimore gazed at me again. He was, I could feel, in a dilemma. From what I knew of him, despite his remarkable absent-mindedness and short-sightedness, he was straight and sensible – and not without a sense of humour; witness his unexpected display of rhyming slang. The chances were, I thought, he was in complete agreement with me. The chances also were that he had his problems with the Library Committee (who had appointed him, and whose blessing he needed constantly to do his job) and that keeping Mrs Bell happy was a valuable aid to him in his dealings with them.

When it came to it, I knew, and he knew, that I would have to go. The only point was, how could we both make it happen with neither side losing face, nor throwing conscience and responsibility to the winds?

"You're not as young as most of the assistants," he began, continuing to gaze steadily at me. "In fact, you've seen more of the world than most of them down there. Bit of university, bit of the City, two years in the R.A.F. With Chiltern or one of the girls or that new chap Eric [Alec], I'd simply tell them to go and that would be the end of it. I don't want to resort to that with you; I'll tell you the situation."

And he proceeded to say more or less exactly what I'd been surmising about to myself; that keeping Mrs Bell at bay was worth a lot to him. "Between you and me, Mrs Bell's a right old bat."

I was much tickled by that description, coming from him.

"But there's a bit more to it than that. Like most awkward people, there's a reason for it. You wouldn't know, but her husband's an invalid. He's got rheumatoid arthritis. Very painful. And a real handful to live with. I think if the truth were known, she'd often rather be out than in. She actually quite likes coming here."

"But she doesn't like going out in the rain?"

"I don't think it's really that either. Sometimes when he's really bad he doesn't like her leaving him. Though she'd hardly tell that to all the library staff." I felt, of course, my resolve weakening. But not before I made one last stand.

"I understand that. And I'm sorry, of course. But it doesn't really alter the situation, does it? After all, there must be many people who come here who could produce a perfectly valid reason why they shouldn't from time to time. And it's only because she is who she is that we go."

The chief agreed that that was perfectly true. But he had another surprise up his sleeve.

"Now, take young Chiltern. And Bill Davies too. I know they both help old people out from time to time by taking books round to them. They don't do it very publicly, but they do do it. Did you know that?"

I knew about Chiltern; not about Bill. The chief went on.

"What I think is – you're perfectly right. She shouldn't expect our assistants to use up their working time, when they should be looking after a number of people, to do it. But presumably you have as much milk of human kindness as the rest of us. You wouldn't object to helping someone out who really needed it, would you? Actually putting yourself out, rather than doing it as part of your official library duties?" Rather self-consciously, I agreed.

"So," he went on, "don't take up library time to do it. Drop the books in on your way home. Then it really becomes a piece of personal help, rather than an unwilling part of your job. What about that?" I felt thoroughly outmanoeuvred. Mortimore may be short-sighted, absent-minded, and vague, but he was no fool. I had no idea he knew about Jim Chiltern's quiet goodwill missions. And I certainly hadn't expected to emerge from that interview not only doing what I had intended not to do, but furthermore to be doing it in my own time.

"Well?" squeaked Beaver, full of interest, as I got downstairs.

"Well?" said Chiltern.

"I'm going," I said, putting on a 'Well-I-was-bound-to-lose-wasn't-I?' face.

159

"But," I added defiantly, "I'm going in my own good time." Which was true, one way or another.

26

A Cat in Plain Covers

One day I came in, to be sent straight out again by
Tovey; re-assigned for two weeks back to the branch
where the famous episode of the hamster had taken
place. My friend Hugh had by now left; moved on to a
more important job in one of the big libraries in Central
London. His assistant David Steel had moved up into
his place, and as yet no-one had arrived to take David's
place in the hierarchy. By virtue of my age and experience (thinking back to the hamster, I wondered
about the experience), I was posted for two weeks as
acting senior assistant. It was to be, Tovey said, "an
interesting experiment".

For about a third of the time I would be there, I
would be in charge. I was sure Tovey would be right; it
would be an interesting experience. Somehow branches
and I had never got on. What should have been a
perfectly peaceful interlude had always somehow turned
into something out of a French farce. I wondered what
fate might have in store this time.

The first thing I discovered was that I had quite
forgotten that this branch, like the others, had not yet
had a photocharger installed; so after nine months I was
suddenly back in the old ticket charging system. And
astonishingly archaic, if rather quieter, it seemed. There
was a total of four on the staff at this branch. David
Steel, me, and two young girls called Moira and Wendy.
Only three of us were on duty at any one time, and more
often than not, it seemed to be the two girls and me. I
soon became aware of a little constraint in the air, which
I put down at first to my newness. But it didn't seem to

go. I was also vaguely aware that one or other of them would disappear from time to time. I didn't think too much about this at first, believing that, new as I was, there must have been things for them to do out of sight which I wouldn't have expected to know about. But, as suspicions grow, it grew.

Out of sheer nosiness, I followed Moira one day when she went off for no apparent reason. She went in the direction of the stockroom – a good deal smaller than our own, with just one wall of shelves and a couple of tables on which preparation of new books was carried out. I slunk along behind Moira towards the stockroom, let her go in, and was just about to go in immediately afterwards, when she executed a beautiful about-turn, and came straight out again.

"Oh," I said, caught walking straight into her.

"Ah," she said, "are you looking for something?" I was, and then again, I wasn't. She was firmly blocking my way. I couldn't think of a reasonable answer at all.

"Er, um," I said, not giving anything away.

She looked at me suspiciously, but decided the best thing to do was to adopt the same approach.

"Mm, yes," she said, and pointedly shut the door in both our faces.

I followed her back to the counter, rather bemused. Clearly something was up, though I couldn't imagine what it could be. If I wanted to, I could of course have just gone into the stockroom and looked around. Somehow, though, Moira's behaviour had made that impossible. As though one couldn't go into a child's room, because she had just announced it wasn't a room at all, but a magic grotto, into which acting senior assistant librarians weren't allowed to go.

"Where's Wendy?" I said suddenly, having realized she was nowhere about.

"She's not here," said Moira unnecessarily.

"I can see that," I said patiently. "What I asked was, *where* is she?"

"She's out."

"But she's not supposed to be out."

"No."

"Well, don't just say no – where is she?"

"Gone to the shop on the corner."

Once again, I got the feeling I shouldn't ask why. But, hang it all, I was in charge, and I had a reasonable right to know where my staff were.

"Come along Moira," I said, hearing myself sound about fifty, "what is going on?"

But before she could answer, Wendy herself crept in. I use the word 'crept' advisedly, because without any doubt there was no better way of describing her entrance. Furtive, silent, trying desperately hard not to look as though she were there at all, Wendy slid through the door without, I swear, opening it more than an inch, and sidled off in the direction of the stockroom. I had had quite enough of this.

Unfortunately, a customer hadn't had quite enough of our service, and decided to choose this moment to present me with a list, written – I was interested to see – in two different coloured inks. (I subsequently discovered this was to differentiate what she considered fiction from non-fiction; a refinement I hadn't met before.) By the time I had dealt with her list, both colours, Wendy had reappeared, looking both breathless and less furtive. Moira raised her eyes inquisitorially at Wendy. Wendy nodded silently back.

I waited until they were both occupied, and stole towards the stockroom. Silently I opened the door, and immediately kicked over a milk-bottle, which had absolutely no right to be there at all. From the speed with which Moira materialized I guessed it was an early warning system.

"Moira," I began again, "what is all this please?" She looked at me all wide-eyed and innocent.

"What is all what?"

"Come along – I wasn't born yesterday. All this keeping me out of the stockroom, and Wendy going shopping, and this – this early warning system?"

"This what?"

"This alarm system."

"Alarm system?"

"Moira," I said, yet again, "something is going on, and I want to hear about it."

Hear about it was exactly what I did, although not in the way either Moira or I had anticipated. What I heard was a sneeze. A very small, well-hidden sneeze, but without any question at all, a sneeze. The sort of sneeze that in my experience came only from small furry coated creatures called cats that had no right, absolutely no right at all, to be sneezing in a library stockroom.

"You've got a cat," I said accusingly. Moira went pink.

"Where is it?"

"Having its tea."

"Well, that wasn't the question I asked, but I'm fascinated by the information. Where is it?" She took me towards one of the tables. Beneath it was an innocent looking pile of books. Which, to my surprise, sneezed again. Moira took the front row of books away, and an extremely small black and white cat looked out at me.

"It's called Rappa," said Moira, without being asked.

"Rappa?"

"It keeps getting dusty from the books," she explained. Or rather, didn't explain.

"I'm sorry, but I don't follow that."

"Dust-wrapper – Rappa" she said, as shamefacedly as she might, producing a pun like that.

I like cats. And I saw no reason not to like this one. I got down on my hands and knees and stroked it.

"You don't mind?" asked Wendy, who had also appeared by now, leaving the counter disgracefully unmanned.

"Why should I mind?"

"Well, we're not really supposed to keep pets here, in the library, are we?" I had to agree.

"But," I went on, "it's not my library. I'm just here to help out. If you've got a cat, you've got a cat. Does

164

David know?" I wished I hadn't asked the question, once I had. I quickly realized that he did know, but that the girls felt they shouldn't say so, in case he got into trouble.

"I'm not going to report it back at headquarters, you know. It's just that if I'm going to be here for another ten days, it would be handy to know just who knows about the cat, and who doesn't."

I felt the need to lighten the level of the conversation, so I went on, "After all, if it sneezes and David's here, I won't know whether to say 'Bless you' or not." I was impressed with that line of argument myself, and was in fact happily smiling at my own joke when I noticed that the two girls were frozen suddenly. Behind me, appearing as he so often did at the critical moment, loomed Tovey.

He looked down at the cat, which carefully timed its next sneeze to coincide with his arrival, ignored it, and turned to me.

"Can you spare me a few moments?" he asked in a serious tone. I glanced at the girls, who clearly had decided I was about to get into trouble on their behalf.

"It really wasn't his fault . . ." Moira began, but Tovey cut her off.

"Come along," he said to me again, "I've got to get straight back."

I followed him into the tiny office, and he shut the door. It seemed he was making an unbelievably serious incident out of a small matter of black and white fluff.

"Have you got *The Carpetbaggers* in?" he asked, slightly pinkly. "My wife's dying to read it, and we've lost the copy at Central."

27

Mortimore's Last Stand

It appeared to be a perfectly ordinary Thursday afternoon. Having said that, I also have to say that Thursday
afternoons were not ordinary in themselves. It was early
closing in that area, and as a consequence, we were
busier than on other afternoons. We got many of the
local shopkeepers in, for one thing. And for another,
people who couldn't go shopping, but still wanted to go
out, came to the library. The net effect was that Thursday afternoons were often quite like Saturday afternoons. In a word, busy.

On this particular Thursday, Chiltern was settled,
unbudgeably, on the 'In' counter; Jill, sleepily, on the
readers' advisory desk; and I, noisily, on the photocharger on the way out. Beaver was off duty; Alec was
off duty; Tovey tucked securely away in his office; Janet
busy around the shelves somewhere; and a small curl of
smoke rising from the stockroom told everyone where
Bill Davies was. The first signs that things might get out
of hand were when three people descended upon Jill at
the enquiry desk simultaneously. The most usual request
was to reserve a book; this took very little time providing
the reader knew what book he or she wanted, and who it
was by. If they didn't – and this time they didn't – it
meant a little research via the catalogue, or in extreme
cases, a journey upstairs to the cataloguing department
for more information.

You can, of course, guarantee that if you have a
queue, it is always the most complicated question you
get asked first – and so it was this time. I saw, with a
slight darkening of my mental horizon, Jill going up-

stairs, with no great speed in her step. She was, I felt, unlikely to come back quickly. No-one seemed to want to go out at that particular moment, so I walked across to the second in the enquiry queue.

"Can I help you?"

"Where's she gone?" That seemed a rather odd request from a reader, and took me by surprise.

"Upstairs," I replied, not very originally.

"I can see that," growled the customer, a heavily-built young man of about twenty-five. There didn't seem much I could add, other than "Upstairs – to our cataloguing department."

"Why?"

"Why?" I echoed, thinking this had already gone quite far enough.

"Why?" came the second echo.

"Well, she's just looking up a book for this lady," and I pointed to that lady.

"How long will she be?"

"I've no idea; five or six minutes perhaps."

"I'll wait."

Thinking it sounded rather like someone waiting for their favourite hairdresser, I shrugged and turned to the third member of the queue, a middle-aged midwife. (I think she was a midwife; she might have been from the Women's Royal Naval Service, but it didn't seem very likely.)

But before I could even ask what she wanted, a sudden loud squawk, followed by catastrophic crying, removed me very suddenly from the counter to part of the non-fiction library, where a small boy had got his hand stuck in one of the bookcases. I couldn't begin to understand how he had done it, and I couldn't ask his mother because she was nowhere to be seen. I set about extracting his hand, to the accompaniment of a stentorian banshee wail.

At this moment, the chief came on the scene, saw the queue at the enquiry desk, saw a queue at the photocharging station, saw Chiltern busy with his own queue coming in. For the first time I had ever known it, Mr Mortimore entered the arena and looked around, deciding where to join in and help.

"Ah," said several voices at him at once.

"Over here," said another one.

"Blimey," said Bill Davies, who had chosen that moment to come out of hiding. But one quick look was enough, and he retreated to the stockroom again.

The chief decided the photocharger was the easiest thing to take over, and sat down gingerly and began to get the thunder and lightning to work. This didn't seem to the taste of the midwife who may have been from the Navy, and she called out in an extremely horsy voice: "I say, Mr Um, I've been waiting some minutes over here you know."

While this was going on, the boy's mother had appeared, and between us we were getting absolutely nowhere towards freeing the child's hand. He, for his part, was having no difficulty at all in keeping up his wail.

"Mr Tovey," the chief called out desperately. Tovey took one look at the situation, picked up the phone, and was apparently deep in conversation within half a second.

Janet, who had observed all, and like the rest of us was thoroughly enjoying the sight of the chief at work publicly for once, felt she could no longer stay away, and hurried over to the counter. Unfortunately she failed to notice the shopping bag of the midwife/WRNS lady, and half-tripped over it. She grabbed the trolley for support, which immediately rolled away, leaving her spread-eagled on the floor.

The chief rushed over to pick her up, went faintly pink at the sight of a good deal more female leg than was seemly for a public library, and held out his hand looking the other way. Janet, who had clearly twisted her ankle severely, clambered to her feet and lurched over to the enquiry desk, where she collapsed white-faced onto the chair. Completely ignoring the fact that

Janet was obviously dazed and in considerable pain, the horsy midwife Naval lady pounced.

"Can you now help me with these books?" she barked at Janet, changing from a horse to a bitch.

Made thoroughly reckless by the recent exposure of Janet's thigh, the chief gave vent to his feeling of outrage that the woman should behave in such a selfish and unsympathetic manner.

"You bloody fool," said Mr Mortimore, "can't you see she's hurt?"

As these challenging words rang round the building, the boy stopped howling, Janet sat up, Chiltern stopped taking books in, and Tovey put down the phone. A splutter from the stockroom told me that the speech had carried as far as Bill Davies too. We all converged on the counter, and Jill descended the stairs in a stately fashion. The midwife stood mouth agape. The chief also stood mouth agape. No-one could have blamed him, but, one had to admit it, it wasn't quite the done thing for the chief librarian to address a respectable middle-aged lady reader in quite those terms.

We all gathered at the counter to see the play-off. The play-off was a little slow in starting, however, largely because the lady in question was so startled she couldn't bring herself to speak. We all waited, fascinated.

"I demand," she said, slowly and deliberately, "to speak to whoever is in charge here."

"I'm in charge here," said the chief, trying desperately to muster up some dignity.

"Yes, well, I find that most hard to believe, and – *Ah . . .!*"

At the "Ah", she looked past us all and we turned to see that her gaze had alighted on the hapless Bill Davies, lurking behind the A–Fs of the fiction. Bill shuddered noticeably, and did his very best to disappear between two large books. Unsuccessfully. The midwife, who had clearly made the usual mistake of taking Bill for the highest authority, stalked up to him (catching him, incidentally, trying to stuff a noticeably burning pipe in his pocket).

"I consider," she said loftily, "the behaviour of your, your . . ." she waved in the direction of the chief, who was looking thoroughly mortified, ". . . your *subordinate* most offensive. I insist that you demand he should apologize to me *now*. At this *instant*."

No-one at all knew what to do. Bill shifted about looking deeply uneasy. Mortimore stood inside the counter, utterly perplexed. Chiltern turned his back on the entire situation, it being all too much for him to take. Janet was on the verge of tears. Jill had retired into a corner of the library with the thick-set man, it was clear what *that* had been about. And I – I was beside myself with interest, wondering how Aristotle would have dealt with the situation. Silence descended, for what seemed like a week and a half. Finally, from behind us came footsteps. Tovey, as he always seemed to be doing, materialized exactly at the crunch point.

"I, in fact, am in charge of the lending library," he said, coolly. "I am perfectly sure, Madam, that you will forgive Mr Mortimore here from speaking out in the heat of the moment. And I am sure Mr Mortimore himself didn't mean to offend you personally. Isn't that so?" Mortimore nodded weakly, at a total loss for the only time since I had known him.

"Will you accept our apology?" said Tovey politely. After a second, the atmosphere crumbled. The woman looked mollified and nodded. The chief mumbled something quite incoherent, and vanished upstairs. Janet started to rub her leg. Bill lit his pipe in full view of everyone. Jill giggled loudly in the corner. Chiltern reopened the 'In' counter. Tovey coolly wandered back to his office. I was just about to set the thunder and lightning in operation again when a high-pitched shriek rent the air. The boy had got his hand stuck again, and his mother was smacking him for good measure.

28

Postscript

Despite the almost daily excitements, of one form or another, that took place in the library, I had been realizing for some time that I still hadn't found the job that suited *me*.

So on 5th November, two years to the day after I had walked in as a member of the staff, I walked out, a member of the public again. Not, however, without a final skirmish with Tovey. Earlier that last day I had walked into his office, to find him and Bill Davies looking at a bottle of wine they had just bought.

"Aha," I thought to myself, "my leaving present. How very nice."

I had a slight feeling of embarrassment at discovering it too soon and so publicly, but I had walked straight into it, and there was no way of pretending I hadn't seen it. I was about to make some sort of comment, like, "I think I probably shouldn't have seen that; we'd better pretend I hadn't", when Tovey looked up casually and said, "Old Stewart's leaving present. Can't send the poor old sod off without something to cheer him up." By coincidence, Mr Stewart the janitor was also leaving the same day; but in his case he was retiring – for the second time.

A quick look round the room told me there was no second bottle lurking – and anyway why should they have hidden just one of them? Obviously, the poor old sod's departure was thought to be of more significance than mine. Most people find it hard to accept that they deserve to be treated as second best, and I was no exception. For the rest of my final day, I went about feeling rather aggrieved.

When the final teatime arrived, and Mr Stewart came up (the only time I had ever known him to do so), I didn't feel any less aggrieved. Tovey made a little speech, and then handed over the wine to Mr Stewart.

He then turned to me, made a little speech, and handed over *my* wine. Just like that. Where he got it from, I have no idea. It had certainly not been standing next to Stewart's bottle under the table. And it had certainly not been in his hand all the time. It had just materialized – just like Tovey himself was always materializing, at the crucial moment.

Where it had been hiding in Tovey's office earlier, I didn't know. *Why* it had been hiding, I didn't know. It was simply Tovey being Tovey, all over. The one thing I did know was that I was going to miss that rather warped dry wit. And, unlike the saying, it wasn't going to be a good miss.